Baby's First Year of Life

Real Advice. No Sugarcoating.

Emma Markey

978-1-917728-24-9

Copyright © 2025 Emma Markey

All rights reserved.

All intellectual property rights, including copyright, design right and publishing rights, rest with the author. No part of this ebook may be copied, reproduced, or transmitted in any way, without the written permission of the author. The information in this book was deemed correct by the author at the time of publication. The author does not assume liability for loss or damage caused by errors or omissions. This is for your personal use only and not meant to replace any medical or professional advice. Published in Ireland by Orla Kelly Publishing.

CONTENTS

About this Book v

Chapter One: Be Prepared 1

Chapter Two: Feeding 13

Chapter Three: Sleep 26

Chapter Four: Milestones 34

Chapter Five: General Tips and what's often
                    overlooked 57

Chapter six: Timeline Breakdown 68

0 – 6 Weeks 70
6 – 12 weeks 79
3 – 6 months 90
6 – 9 months 100
9 – 12 months 114

Final Note 121

About This Book

Whether you're reading this with a baby snoozing on your chest, a toddler tugging at your leg, or in those rare, quiet moments when you finally get to sit down—welcome. I wrote this book for you.

Let me introduce myself. I'm a stay-at-home mum to two little girls, Anna and Molly, who are just 16 months apart. Life in our house is a beautiful, chaotic whirlwind of giggles, tantrums, and endless snack requests. But this wasn't always the plan. Before becoming a mum, I worked full-time as a social worker, specialising in disability services and child protective services. When my first daughter was born, I fully intended to return to work part-time. But life had other plans. My husband's job required frequent travel, and by the time I was ready to go back, we were already expecting baby number two. So, I made the decision to stay home and embrace the mayhem of raising two under two.

Oh, and did I mention I'm also Type 1 diabetic? Pregnancy for me meant countless hospital appointments and strict blood sugar control. It wasn't easy, but it shaped my perspective on motherhood: balancing the chaos with structure, finding joy in the little moments, and learning to adapt when life throws you curveballs.

Why I Wrote This Book

Motherhood is the hardest, most rewarding job you'll ever have. There's no manual, no training, and no performance reviews to tell you how you're doing. But there's also nothing that compares to the unconditional love you feel for your child. It's overwhelming, beautiful, and, let's be honest, sometimes downright exhausting.

When I was pregnant with my first daughter, I did what most of us do—I researched. I read books, scoured the internet, and asked every mum I knew for advice. But what I found was often vague or incomplete. Everyone said things like, "Once you get into a sleep routine…" or "Once they're on a feeding schedule…" but no one told me *how* to get there. I was left piecing together bits of information, feeling like I was constantly playing catch-up.

That's why I wrote this book. I wanted to create the resource I wish I had during those early days—a straightforward, practical guide to navigating your baby's first year. This isn't a one-size-fits-all manual, and I'm not here to tell you that my way is the only way. Every baby is different, and every mum's journey is unique. But I hope that by sharing what worked for me, I can help you find your own path with a little more confidence and a lot less stress.

What You'll Find in This Book

This book is all about simplifying the first year of motherhood. I'll walk you through everything from feeding schedules to bedtime routines, starting as early as six weeks. Each chapter is designed to guide you through a specific stage of your baby's development, offering practical tips and real-life insights.

My approach is rooted in consistency and long-term structure. I believe in starting as you mean to go on—introducing routines early so they become second nature for both you and your baby. For example, I started bedtime routines with both of my girls at six weeks old. It wasn't about rigid schedules but about creating a sense of predictability and calm in our day-to-day lives.

I'll also share the little things that often get overlooked—like the equipment I found most useful, how to support your baby's developmental milestones, and the role you play in teaching them about the world. Babies are like little sponges, soaking up everything they see and hear from the moment they're born. I believe learning starts on day one, and I'll show you how I approached this with my own girls.

This isn't a guidebook, and it's not about perfection. It's about sharing my experiences—the good, the messy, and everything in between—in the hope that it makes your journey a little easier. Trust your instincts, because no one knows your baby better than you. A mother's intuition is a power all its own.

So, if you've ever found yourself thinking, "Why didn't anyone tell me this?"—this book is for you. Let me share the insider tips, the lessons learned, and the moments that made me laugh (and cry) along the way.

You've got this. And I'm here to help.

With love,
Emma

CHAPTER ONE

BE PREPARED

I am going to start with the simpler side of things, the shopping list. Babies are cute and all, but they require a lot of equipment. However, the good thing about this technological era is that it can make life with a baby run a lot smoother. So, let's dive into the essentials you'll need to make the first year with your baby a little easier. Here's a list of items that I found invaluable, along with some tips based on my experiences.

- **Travel System aka Pram and Car Seat**

    A travel system is essential for getting around with your baby, and there are plenty of options to choose from. If you're planning to have children close in age, consider a model that can convert into a double pram/stroller. We overlooked this with Anna, and by the time

Molly arrived, we needed to invest in a new pram. As for car seats, they're a must-have from day one; you'll need one to leave the hospital. Choose one that suits your needs and budget.

- **Baby Camera/Monitor**

    Initially, you will not need a monitor however, once the baby is older, you will want a monitor to check in on the baby while they are napping/sleeping. Majority are portable, so you can bring them with you to the bath/shower, carry out household duties or watch TV at the end of the day. What I loved was that ours read the temperature of the room, which is fantastic for safe sleeping. We changed our monitor to a dual camera model once I was pregnant with Molly. Again keep this in mind if you are purchasing a monitor and think you may have two children close in age.

- **Co-sleeping Crib**

    This item is a lifesaver as they enable your baby to sleep in their own bed from day one (key), whilst also giving them and you the comfort of sleeping next to you. It aligns or attaches to your bed, allowing the baby to sleep level with you. Research shows how tightly bound the psychological and social aspects of the mother and baby relationship really are and through sleeping 'safely' side by side, this relationship is aided and strengthened. A co-sleeping crib allows you to sleep beside your baby, lean over and easily pick them up when feeding at night. It is also a great help during your post-partum recovery period. It is a much safer way for you and your baby to sleep. I have never taken either of my children into my bed, this is what most referred to as 'bed sharing'. Bed sharing is the single highest risk factor for sudden infant death syndrome (SIDS), and that is why I choose to co-sleep with both my children. National Childbirth Trust (NCT) states that *"having your baby in their own bed in your room is the safest way for them to sleep, and the next-to-me crib allows this".* You're advised for the baby to sleep in your bedroom for the first 6 months, so like everything, I will advise, start as you mean to go on. If they have always slept in their own bed, then there is nothing to change/introduce later. I found my children's transition to their own room a lot easier than the majority (if not all) of my friends.

- **Black Out Curtains**

    These are a must as babies are so sensitive to light. When initially teaching them the difference between night and day (yes, day and night confusion is a thing, I will tell you how I avoided that too), I did not use the blackout curtains for naps. But for the last bottle and bedtime, they are so necessary. You will require blackout curtains for their own room. There is no getting around the long day's aka sunshine until 10pm during the summer months. We further ended up getting temporary blackout blinds (suction cups which stick onto the window) to try and double up on the curtains.

- **Sleep Bags**

    Temperature is the one thing I really obsessed over with Anna and never more so than at night. Sleep bags are a great option for safe sleeping. The Lullaby Trust offers the following advice, "baby sleeping bags are a good option as they prevent your baby's head from being covered by wriggling under the bedding". Now there is a big push to swaddle newborns, before they become more mobile. I found neither of my girls liked to be swaddled, and to be honest, they were always mobile with their arms, legs usually moving around from about week 2. So, sleep bags are a great alternative, and many children remain in sleep bags until 2+ years old, so nothing new to introduce later. You can choose different togs for different seasons to help keep your little one at the right temperature. Optimal room temperature is advised to be between 16 – 20 degrees Celsius. As well as being a safer sleep option, they can also help prevent potential wake-ups from the baby getting feet stuck between cot bars once they are a little older and a lot more mobile.

- **Night Light**

    I found a dimmer night light most useful as you could adjust the brightness as needed. I used one with a timer, so when I started the last night feed (when bedtime routine was introduced, we'll get to that at week 6), I would start the one-hour timer at the beginning of the bottle. It also allows you to see the baby during night feeds without overstimulating the baby with overhead or bedside lighting.

- **Sound Machine**

    Sticking with sleep aids, a sound machine is your best friend. Whether it's white noise or heartbeat, this will help soothe the baby in their crib, especially at the beginning. The sound mimics womb sounds and creates a comfortable and familiar environment, which helps the baby feel secure. Many also have a sensor motion which you can choose to leave on, so if the baby begins to wake, it will come on automatically.

- **Echo Dot**

    Although I used a sound machine teddy with both girls in the co-sleeping crib as soon as they were in their own rooms (6 months), I would feed and put them into their cot beds with instrumental lullabies playing. You can also switch to white/pink noise through the night if/when required in the transition period of moving into their own room. I will discuss this in detail in the 6-9 month chapter.

- **Changing Stations**

  One in your bedroom and one in your main living/day area. Babies need their nappy changed numerous times throughout the day, so if you can set up more than one changing station, it will make life easier.

- **Baby Bouncer/Seat/ Mat**

  All or either of these are great for the baby to stay safe and comfortable for times when you need to make food/answer the door/pee. Also great for baby's 'wake windows'. Many options can adapt with the baby's age, so whichever option you like, go with it.

- **Baby Carrier/Wearer**

  I easily used our baby carrier up to 12 months, they are fantastic for bonding, soothing and getting about with the baby at all stages. Also fantastic for 'witching hour' (we'll get to that). There are many options and prices available, so whichever works for you, but it's a top purchase in our house.

- **Gripe Water** (teething/wind)

    This is an herbal supplement available over the counter in pharmacies. It can be used as an aid for infant gas, colic, teething and hiccups. This worked brilliantly for Anna, as she had silent reflux (basically baby heartburn). I did have it with Molly, but she did not seem to need it. If the baby is prone to hiccups or gas, this can provide relief.

*TIP: Can dip doe-dee (pacifier) into Gripe Water or pour measured amount into bottle teat to aid consumption.

- **Teething Products**

    I remember being so surprised at how early my daughters both showed signs of teething. Signs can start as early as 3 months or as late as 12 months. Both Anna and Molly began showing signs of teething at 3 months, and I did not want to jump straight to paracetamol/ibuprofen due to their age. But also because you are so limited in what medication you can give to babies/children. I did not feel comfortable medicating a baby so young. So, there are many different products available, but Anna responded best to homeopathic teething powders and teething gels. With Molly, it was Anbesol, which is a liquid you rub onto the gums to help relieve pain and discomfort.

Teething Rings were also brilliant with both girls, especially when they got a little older and were developing their motor skills and hand-eye coordination. You can place the teething rings into the fridge/freezer beforehand, which adds a little instant relief.

*TIP: you can place doe-dee's and/or bottle teats in the freezer to use for quick teething pain relief.

- **Pain Relief**

    Infant paracetamol and/or ibuprofen are a staple in the medicine cupboard. But I'll be honest, it was my last go-to, not for any other reason than I didn't want to be too quick to medicate in any situation. However, depending on the time of year you have your baby, you may reach for these items sooner than you think. With Anna (spring baby), she did not get sick until about 10 months, with Molly (autumn baby), 7 weeks!

*TIP: The bottle teat works wonders for aiding baby's consumption of oral medication also, again measure contents in a syringe and then put into bottle teat once in baby's mouth. Also, you may need a larger size teat, depending on the liquid density.

- **Vapour Plug-ins**

    Are a new level of amazing when cold/flu season kicks in and baby is congested. I use lavender and/or chamomile scented, you simply plug into a wall socket in your/baby's room if they are bunged up, i.e. runny nose, stuffy nose. The vapour fills the room to help clear their airways and ease their breathing.

General:
- Nappies
- Wipes
- Nappy Cream
- Muslins and Bibs
- Formula (if not breastfeeding)
- Flask – for bottle on the go
- Rocking Chair

- Pacifier – Doe-dee in my house – if you want.
- Baby Grows and Onesies
- Hats/Socks/Mittens (depending on the season the baby is born)

If you choose to bottle feed, which I did with both Anna and Molly, as I am Type 1 Diabetic and well it was a natural choice for me not to breastfeed. Do not be afraid to choose how to feed your baby. I know we are pushed to breastfeed, 'breast is best' and all that, but honestly, I had no desire to try. Do what feels natural to you and do not allow anyone to make you feel guilty for your choice!

> Tip: Keep a head of cabbage in the fridge. It works wonders on hard swollen breasts.

Day 5 postpartum, your breasts are going to be bigger and more painful than ever before; I'm not taking period pain tenderness here, I'm talking rock hard, swollen breasts. I remember standing in my kitchen the morning of day 5, about to leave to bring Anna to the hospital for her midwife check, and my friend, let's call her Samantha, appearing at the side door with a head of cabbage. Samantha asked how my boobs where, when I replied 'fine', she told me "They won't be later, put this in the fridge then onto your boobs, you can thank me later", and with that she was gone. On the way back from the hospital appointment my breasts felt like they were going to explode. I got home, got the cabbage from the fridge, and my God, the relief! As unusual as it sounds, the cabbage leaves absorb some of the fluid from the glands within the breast area, reducing the fullness in the tissue. So, if you take nothing else from this book, take the cabbage hack.

To aid with your shopping I have created a QR code below to reach my website where many of the items I have mentioned can be purchased:

CHAPTER TWO

FEEDING

As this book is about my personal journey, I will not delve into breastfeeding advice. If you choose to breastfeed, fantastic, it is a personal choice for every woman. For me, I chose to bottle-feed both my girls, and I am excited to share what I have learned along the way. Therefore, I will only discuss bottle feeding, where to start, what you'll need on your feeding journey and how I established a feeding routine.

What you need – more equipment –

- A bottle kit – the choices are endless, but ultimately, you'll need:
  3 x 270ml bottles
  2 x 150ml bottles
  2 x level 1 teats

3 x level 2 teats

2 x level 3 teats

My kit came with the steam sterilising unit, one which you placed in the microwave. Research what version of steam sterilisation you wish to use and go with that.

- Bottle brush – to clean after feeding, before the bottle is sterilised.
- Washing up liquid – to complete said cleaning.
- Bottle prep machine: A later product I used from about week 3 with Anna was a bottle prep machine. People had mentioned them to me, but I didn't see the value in it until baby arrived. Now with Molly, the same prep machine is still going strong. It is a great help, as prior to purchasing one, we were relying on the old technique of boiling the kettle 30 mins before a feed was due, and this was not as simple as it sounds. Anna had silent reflux, so until this was addressed with prescription medication, she was only finding relief from her discomfort when feeding. Which meant a lot of bottles close together, so the kettle was quickly replaced with the bottle prep machine. Now I need to note that the

NHS does not recommend same. However, what you will learn is that there are a lot of things not recommended, whether that be by a health care professional or family/friend's recommendations, so you will have to ultimately decide for yourself.

- You will need to choose a Formula; all contain similar ingredients, so again the choice is yours. With Anna, we changed the formula a few times initially due to her seemingly being hungry. However, once her reflux had been diagnosed and she began her prescription, we settled on one and immediately fed Molly the same without issue.

- Bottle teats: One thing I didn't know prior to having babies is that there are different sizes of bottle teats. With Anna, she needed to change size (go from teat size number 1 to number 2), the standard every three months. However, with Molly, she was a bigger baby, so on her 10-day health check, the midwife advised we change to a level 2 teat. This worked great, and so she moved teat size every three months thereafter. Keep this in mind and/or ask your midwife/health visitor about the same.

How much should the baby be eating

All formulas provide guidelines for age and quantity of formula on the package. As with everything though, all babies are different. Anna was a smaller baby, but she always had a greater appetite than Molly. So, start with the guidelines but don't panic or put too much pressure on meeting exact oz's.

The good thing with bottle feeding is that you know exactly how much your baby is eating. Your baby will be reviewed by both midwives and health visitors initially, and you can discuss any worries or concerns with them. Your baby is weighed at each health check, therefore any issues can be flagged.

Winding/Burping

Winding was a challenge, especially with Anna, who seemed to hate every position we tried. I remember one night, after what felt like hours of trying, I finally found a technique that worked for her. So don't give up if it's tough at first. Every baby is different, and you'll find what works. There are different positions advised for winding so try out different techniques and see which baby responds best to. For example, over the shoulder, across the lap, sitting on your lap, you can also try them on their back and gently massage their tummy or moving legs back and forth like a bicycle motion (this one also helps with gas). You can view any of these online or ask a healthcare professional to demonstrate prior to the baby's hospital discharge.

Initially, bottles will take anything up to 40 mins, depending on baby's appetite and temperament. With Anna, she was always a quick eater, with Molly, a different story. But both were terrible to wind, and what I cannot stress enough is to not overlook winding, I'm talking 15-20 mins in the early days. The first few weeks, I was advised to wind every oz drank. I did this initially with both girls to very little avail. So, by about week 2, I would wind halfway through a feed or when baby showed signs of wind during a bottle. Crying, squirming, or simply stopping a feed are easy signs of wind. I made this change as I found both would get more agitated by pausing every oz, so I moved winding to halfway and the end of a bottle. This is trial and error, and until the baby is here, you cannot be sure what will work. However, once a bottle was finished, I would wind both for 15-20 mins until they were 6 months old. Neither would burp that much, but if I tried placing them down sooner, it always ended in cries due to discomfort. Some babies wind more easily than others, mine simply did not. But I think even being held upright for the winding period eased any discomfort.

Routine: Establishing a feeding routine was a lifesaver for me. It helped bring some order to the chaos of those early months. Of course, there were days when everything went out the window, but having a plan to fall back on made an enormous difference. I will break down implementing a feeding routine, pushing time between bottles and everything else in the timeline breakdown.

Weaning (6 months)

Where to begin…Equipment…again:

- Highchair – if you can get one which pulls up/onto your table, even better.
- Full body bibs – painters' overall style
- Bowl/Plates – with suction cups on base
- Baby utensils – I placed the same with every meal from the beginning.
- Baby cup – multiple versions. Use it as you wish, again placed with every meal from the beginning.
- For cooking, you can get a blender, but with the majority of foods, apart from soup, a fork will work just fine.
- And the more wipes, the better

Once the baby can sit independently and hold their head up, it is recommended to start solid foods, usually this aligns with month 6. Signs to look out for if unsure whether baby is ready to begin weaning include showing less interest in bottle feeding, watching and/or reaching for what you are eating. From 6-month babies require a minimum of 500ml of formula, so depending on the number and size of bottles, you can replace bottles with food. I did not replace any bottle feed for food immediately, I introduced food initially between bottles, then at 8months began replacing bottles with food. First time weaning is scary, there is no point in saying otherwise. With Anna, I initially began spoon feeding but quickly moved onto finger foods. With Molly, she honestly showed no interest in spoon feeding and wanted to self-feed from the beginning, so we did. I will provide a breakdown of how I weaned both girls in the timeline breakdown.

You can start how you feel comfortable, there are two methods of weaning commonly used, Spoon Feeding and Baby Led Weaning BLW. Just to note, you can introduce water for the baby to drink at this point (6 months) however, you must boil tap water before baby drinks it from 6 to 12 months, as it is not deemed sterile straight from the tap. Bottled water is also not recommended due to possible sodium levels.

I found the easiest way to do this was to boil the kettle along with the first bottle, then place boiled water into a pouring jug and then into the fridge. That way, you have a reserve for mealtimes throughout the day and don't need to remember ahead of time. Currently, there is no recommended amount of water for babies to drink in the UK, so do not worry too much about the same.

Also, it is important that you know the signs of choking before weaning. First time weaning is scary, regardless of how you do it, so know the difference between baby gagging and choking. Gagging is common, especially at the beginning, as it is the baby's own safety response to food travelling too far back into the mouth, and it is very different to choking. A baby who is gagging will make a little noise and appear to be mildly coughing. A child who is choking will be unable to breathe, or might gasp and/or wheeze, make no noise and look terrified/panicked. They can also have a bluish colour of the lips/face. This is terrifying, I know, but all choking hazards can be minimised through the preparation of food (softness) and serving size (ring-finger thickness). Completing an infant CPR class is also a great option for anyone, regardless of their stage of parenting.

Baby-Led-Weaning BLW

This is a more recent method of weaning, but is quickly picking up in popularity with parents. The approach is to allow your baby to feed themselves finger food (solid food) from the beginning, bypassing purees and mashed foods. BLW encourages fine motor skill development through self-feeding and hand-eye coordination. It enables babies to develop their ability to chew and swallow food, and how much they eat, preventing overfeeding by parents. Some research has shown that as baby has control over the amount of food being consumed and the speed at which they are eating through BLW, this could help reduce the risk of childhood obesity. As baby has control over the food, they can self-regulate and notice their hunger or fullness levels quicker, which could result in a lower chance of becoming overweight compared to children who have been spoon-fed. BLW enables a wider variety of flavours and textures to be tried from the beginning which some research has shown could prevent picky/fussy eating later in life. It also allows babies to try allergen foods earlier, which research now shows that introducing allergens sooner rather than later can be more beneficial for babies. Obviously if there are allergies in your immediate family, you need to be very careful introducing the same. The rule of thumb when introducing any high-risk food is to give it to the baby early in the day to allow time and response to any reaction. And then for three days consecutively to ensure the baby has no issue with the food, e.g. peanut butter, eggs, strawberries. BLW can also make mealtimes easier, as you can introduce food that the entire family is eating.

Now, there are downsides to everything. Some of the negative aspects of BLW include mess and food waste. Initially, food is everywhere, as a baby is once again learning a new skill, food will be on the face, arms, legs, and the floor, which equals the food waste. But over time, the mess and waste will lessen as the baby's appetite and skills develop. It can be more difficult to tell how much the baby is eating, like I said, it's messy. However I found that introducing finger food two/three pieces at a time made it easier to know how much the baby was eating. It can be more time-consuming, as you are allowing the baby control over food intake and the speed which they are eating, so it can take longer than spoon-feeding. However, I did find that by baby eating 'cleaner' and in shorter periods of time, it was easy to gauge their development and improvement at mealtimes. You could physically see the difference in food waste and on the clock.

If you choose to wean through the BLW approach, there are a few things to keep in mind. Initially, you will continue to bottle/breastfeed while introducing solid foods. I will explain how I replaced bottle feeds with food within the timeline breakdown of the baby's first year. But babies continue to get most of their nutrition from formula or breast milk until the age of 1. Eat together, if you can get a highchair which pulls up to your table, perfect. A lot of time and supervision goes into weaning, so making the highchair part of your table is much nicer and easier managed for you. It is also safer, reducing choking hazards, and they can learn from watching you eat. Prepare all foods according to the baby's age. The food size for the baby changes over time, you begin with food size the same as your ring finger and soft enough that you can break the food between your thumb and small finger to reduce the chances of choking.

Spoon-feeding

Spoon-feeding is the more traditional approach when you offer a baby mashed/pureed food on a spoon, progressing to thicker mashed foods. The main difference between spoon-feeding and BLW is the order babies learn feeding skills. With spoon feeding, you control the amount of food the baby has and the timeframe they eat it in. With BLW, the baby decides how much they eat and when to stop. With spoon feeding, you offer the spoon and the baby swallows, with BLW, the baby picks up and chews, developing motor skills sooner. With spoon feeding, you are advised to begin finger foods around 9 months of age, so it is delaying the same process, but depending on your confidence and baby's abilities, the choice is yours. With spoon-feeding, it is important to progress to appropriate textures to help develop the oral and motor skills the baby needs. Staying on thin, watery purees for too long can make the transition to finger foods harder, and the baby can develop a dislike for food textures.

Benefits of spoon-feeding can include more control over the nutrient intake, as parental control over the baby's food intake means less food ending up on the floor. Therefore, less mess is involved compared to BLW. As spoon feeding involves pureed or mashed food, there is less risk of choking, so parents can be more relaxed at the beginning. It can also be easier to know how much the baby is eating, as again, you are in control, and food is only on a spoon. However, this method can slow the baby's development of self-regulating hunger and/or fullness cues as the baby is not deciding how much to eat. It also slows the development of self-feeding until finger foods are introduced at 9 months.

As you can see, the downside for both methods is similar, but the benefits are easily outweighed, especially with aiding the baby's development, so I choose to BLW with both girls. Research shows there is no significant difference in the nutrient intake of either BLW or spoon-feeding if the baby is provided with appropriate foods. It was easier to introduce foods that the entire family were eating sooner and encourage motor skill development as self-feeding strengthens muscles and develops coordination. Now there are still adaptations made to how you cook and serve finger foods in the beginning so that the food is soft enough for the baby to chew. Cut into sizes that reduce choking risk. So, research both methods before the baby reaches 6 months and decide which approach you feel more comfortable with, there are no issues with using a combination of both approaches.

CHAPTER THREE

SLEEP

Believe it or not, this is the most straightforward chapter. Let me share some not-so-common knowledge with you because, despite what we've been told, babies need sleep. As I have stated previously, everything is brand new to babies, they need sleep to process these new experiences and to aid their development. Everyone requires sleep for development, and despite what everyone tells us, 'Good luck getting to sleep for the next three years', babies are no different. Babies are born without an established circadian rhythm (knowing the difference between day & night), and it will only be developed when they reach 3 or 4 months old. This is why helping the baby to differentiate between day and night is crucial in the first three months. I have advised how to do so in the 0-6 weeks timeline breakdown.

It is crucial to teach the baby the difference between day and night sleep in the first year. Even in this first year sleep plays an important role in your child's development. Including physical growth, cognitive development, such as language, memory and executive function. Research has shown that limited deep sleep for infants can be linked to obesity later in life. As sleep deprivation is associated with an increase in the hunger hormone ghrelin. Difficulty sleeping during infancy has been linked with future problems during early childhood, which in turn are linked to learning and behavioural problems. Despite what we hear, research recommends that babies sleep a duration of 14–17 hours a day from birth to three months, 12–15 hours per day for 4 to 11 months and then 11–14 hours a day for infants aged 1 to 2 years.

Now that's the science behind why babies need sleep, but I will tell you how I got there with both my girls by 6 months of age. And no, I was not 'lucky', or they both just happened to be 'good sleepers'. I put the work and consistency of getting a sleep and nap routine in from the start. I believe eating and the general environment have a massive part to play with establishing a baby's sleep routine. My method requires repetition and consistency, it is not difficult, but it is consistent. My sleep routine with the girls began from week 6 and continues still with both 2+ years on. Elements change, which I'll discuss in the timeline breakdown over the months, but the general layout remains the same.

Now everything is guesswork and a balancing act in the beginning. What helps with sleep is knowing your baby's sleep cues, wake windows, and just knowing them better. You can begin a sleep routine from Day 1 however, I was in too much of a newborn haze, both times around. So, I began implementing a sleep routine with both girls at six weeks old. I found by this stage I could read their cries and ques easier (not always) and had the energy to begin. Plus, I found that until the girl's feeding routine was established, it was more difficult to develop their sleep/nap schedule, so my experience is that both go hand in hand.

Sleep Routine

In the early days, 6 weeks to 6 months, I would decrease noise within the home from around 5/5:30 pm, no TV, no music. To try and create a more calming atmosphere in the build-up to bedtime. At the beginning, 6-12 weeks, you are introducing the idea of bedtime. There will most likely be night feeds after the 'bedtime bottle', but what you start now continues throughout the baby's first year.

I would go up to the bedroom before bringing the baby, close the blinds and curtains and have only the night light on. I would have their nappy and a change of clothes ready and play instrumental lullabies in the room. I would tell baby, 'It's bedtime' and repeat the same going up the stairs. My speech would be calm and slower paced than general conversation during the day (but then I talk fast, so you may not need to address this). When we got to the room I would continue speaking to baby. Talk about what you're doing, 'new nappy for bed', 'need to get your jammies on for sleep', place baby in their sleep bag (season depending) and place them into their crib. Once in the crib I would tell baby, 'bedtime, mummy going to get your bottle, be back in a minute'. When I returned, there was no talking, the night light was on its lowest setting, and music continued to play softly. Once their bottle was finished, I would burp the baby for 15 minutes, then say 'bedtime' and place them into the crib. Switch on their sound machine to white noise or heartbeat and leave.

It was never my intention for the baby to be asleep before I put them into their crib, as I wanted them to be used to going into their bed awake. Now, not every night is easy, some nights, a lot more settling is required, but I tried not to lift the baby back out of the crib. I would place my hand on their stomach to comfort them and count to 100 in my head then leave, sit outside the door and wait. At different stages of a baby's first year, getting to sleep or staying asleep will change, and I will discuss the same throughout the timeline breakdown. At this point, I am providing the approach and general technique I used with both girls

For general settling, I would go back in and place my hand on the baby's stomach, provide doedee, count to 100, then leave, repeat if necessary. Once older 6+ months, I would return, place the baby onto their back if they were sitting, say 'bedtime', place a hand on the stomach count to 100 and leave. Through the night, I found that Molly would lose her doedee and look for same more than Anna did. At these times, I would go in, find doedee, place Molly on her back, repeat 'bedtime' and leave. Unless either of the girls was teething or sick, my approach has never changed. Anna slept through the night from week 9, and Molly slept through the night from week 11.

Now the other thing often overlooked is that bedtime begins with morning routine and nap schedule, all of which I introduced at 6 weeks. At this age, I began lifting both girls at 7 am for their morning feed. Now let me be clear at this age I may have done a bottle at 5:45/6 am but I still lifted them at 7 am. It may feel like it will kill you, but we are aiming for the long run people. The difference being if there was an earlier bottle it was done as a night feed, limited interaction, no talking and minimal light. When I lifted them at 7 am, I would open the curtains, change their nappy and put music on to introduce the idea of 'morning'. As they got older, I would push them as close to 7 am, which I will detail in the timeline breakdown.

Hopefully by 6/8 weeks you are beginning to recognise baby's wake windows, sleep cues and the difference in their cries. This will help massively in establishing a nap and sleep schedule. Baby will sleep a lot in the first few weeks, but once their wake windows lengthen, you can begin to introduce morning and afternoon naps. In the morning, Molly was ready for sleep by 9 am, Anna was 9:30 am. As I said, knowing your baby's wake windows and sleep cues really comes in handy from here. For the morning nap, I always changed their clothes prior and told them, 'Mummy is going to get dressed, you have a wee snooze'. For the afternoon nap, both my girls went for their nap 1-3/3:30pm (and still do). The approach to the afternoon nap was like bedtime in that they had a bottle before, about 10 mins of play, then upstairs for 'naptime'. The only thing usually recommended that I didn't do was to darken the room during the morning/afternoon nap. I was more interested in defining naps and bedtime, so I did not pull either of the girls' curtains at naptimes until they were in their own rooms from 6 months of age.

*TIP - label each sleep period differently. For morning nap 9/9:30 am it was 'little snooze', afternoon nap 'naptime' and bedtime 'bedtime'. I don't know if this really made a difference, but I felt by attaching a different term for each period helped the girls to recognise which sleep they were going for, but who knows. All I can say is that even now, Anna knows the morning snooze (which she now plays in her room during) is so 'mummy can get showered and dressed', the afternoon is 'nap' and bedtime is 'bedtime'.

As I said, consistency and routine help with all aspects of a baby's development, but especially with getting good sleep. Now I know some will advise not to use sleep aids such as doedee's, but I didn't have the energy for every battle. Both girls used a doedee for sleep, shoot me. I will discuss the highs and lows of sleep regressions and a more detailed response to settling the girls through the timeline, but honestly, I did not have a traumatic experience with sleep. By 12 weeks, I was getting a full night's sleep and a solid nap in the day. I did not 'sleep train' my children. I simply introduced a routine early and stuck with it. Even when there were times of resistance, it was short-lived, and no one suffered. The good thing about sleep routines is that it can help you tell when baby is teething or becoming unwell. As the routine is disrupted, and you can figure out the reason for the same quickly.

CHAPTER FOUR

MILESTONES

Baby's first year comes with rapid growth, learning and developmental milestones. This is a very exciting time for both you and your baby! As you adapt to your new role as mummy, whether this be your first or third baby, your baby is adapting to their new environment. Baby will be monitored and reviewed closely by their healthcare provider to ensure their growth is consistent and healthy within their first year. And to ensure they are meeting milestones within certain timeframes of their first year. Remember, babies develop at their own pace, and these milestones are simply a list of what you can expect. If at any point you are concerned about your child's development, contact your healthcare provider, who will review and decide whether further intervention is required to support your baby. But try not to panic if the baby isn't meeting every milestone within a specific timeframe. Babies can reach certain milestones sooner and others later.

Baby's First Month

The first month with your little bundle is both draining and amazing. If this is your first baby, give yourself time for the life adjustment. Baby will predominantly, sleep, eat, poop and sleep again, especially the first two weeks. With 'wake windows' only being about 45-60 mins. Baby will be getting stronger quickly, she may be able to lift her head for a short time when held. Tummy time is an important activity for your baby at this stage, and your healthcare provider will be encouraging you to do the same every day. Tummy time is simply placing the baby on their stomach for short intervals and allowing them to try and lift their head. It is to help their neck and back muscle development, and you will most likely hate it. They seem so small and helpless, and both of mine hated it, but it is a necessity. Don't put too much pressure on yourself or your baby at this early stage, but try just 20-30 seconds, building up over time. Neither of my girls particularly enjoyed tummy time. But I found that once they were a little older, doing the same on a play mat or using a baby mirror whilst they were on their stomachs helped with their movement of lifting their heads, eventually onto their elbows and hands.

Sight and hearing will develop quickly in this first month, babies respond best to black-and-white images and vibrant colours at this stage. Baby will begin to be more aware of their surroundings. Including recognising your voice and may react with startle at a loud noise. Half of babies begin showing signs that they recognise their main caregivers as early as the first month. They may respond differently to you than they do to strangers, such as making eye contact with you or quietening down when you come back into the room. Your baby will have learned to focus with both eyes and may now start tracking objects. For example, a toy passed in front of their face, or you can move your face towards and back from theirs, maintaining eye contact. Their eyes may lock onto yours.

Grasp response, this is when the baby automatically closes her fingers around yours when you touch their palm. This reflex is strongest within the first 8 weeks of the baby's life, and your heart will melt every time it happens.

It's never too early to start talking or singing to a baby, I would just narrate everything, changing nappies, getting dressed and tell her what every random object was. When the baby was in the carrier, I would walk around the house pointing at household objects telling her, 'that's the kettle, it boils water', 'that's the washing machine, it cleans clothes', whatever you want. This is also great when walking in the pram or grocery shopping. We have no idea how much is registering in their little brains, but it can do no harm. Books are also a great way to talk to a baby, now obviously they've no idea what a book is, but never too early to start. You can also get fantastic picture books beginning from no age and many with high contrast colours, so it's a great way of introducing books to babies. Music is also great at this time, whether you are singing nursery rhymes or playing your favourite artist.

Baby may begin to ohh and ahh this early, repeat the same back. When the baby takes a break from babbling, simply respond with a similar noise. This introduces the first idea of speech, plus it's adorable, and you'll just want to do it.

That's a lot more than you thought it would be, I know.

Baby's Second Month

Baby can, I don't think either of mine did this early, but apparently, they can smile at this age. If it does happen, you will forget every poonami and sleepless night you've had.

Baby's sight is developing past two-colour preferences, so provide a variety of objects, different shapes and colours to look at and touch. Soft balls and cloth picture books are perfect. Baby's movements are still sporadic at this point, with not much coordination between arm and leg movements. They are beginning to develop smoother movement, and I found a great way of helping this was with jingle cuffs placed on the baby's arms and legs. This helps them to explore their body parts with the help of sound, and it's just a great way to pass time during the baby's wake window. Which will normally have increased to 1-2 hours at this stage.

Baby will receive a 6-8 week health check. This is when your health visitor will review the baby's weight, length and head circumference. They will also check the baby's eyes, heart, hips and genitals. They will also ask about the baby's feeding and advise on the baby's first immunisations (6, 12 and 16 weeks).

On average, babies will experience a growth spurt around week 6, which can result in more feedings, baby being fussier and more demanding. Don't stress too much, it's too early to have established anything close to routine, and this increased hunger and fussiness should pass quickly.

Baby's Third Month

A lot more babbling by this stage, so continue to narrate your day with your baby. It is a very simple way to support language development. By this stage babies' wake windows are longer (75 mins to 2.5 hours). They'll be by your side for the majority of tasks you are completing, so you may as well chat while you do them.

You may notice the baby placing her feet on you or the floor when holding them up. Let a little of their weight onto their legs and see if they push back up. Baby should be bringing both hands together, playing with their fingers and open fists. Hand-eye coordination is developing, so continue to hold toys close to the baby's face, and they may begin to bat at it or grasp it.

Tummy time should have improved by now, with the baby possibly starting to lift their head and chest, mimicking a push-up. This is where toys and baby mirrors are great for supporting tummy time. Both Anna and Molly did a lot better with tummy time on a play mat at this stage. Head control is usually a lot better at this stage, with the baby being able to lift their head while lying on their back. Or if sitting supported, hold their head steady. All babies are different, both my girls had begun doing the same at week 6. Again, do not panic too much about not falling into exact milestone brackets.

Baby can roll over as early as now, both my girls were closer to 4 months before they rolled over. Neither did it with any warning, so be prepared. You may want to start changing nappies on the floor from this point as once the baby rolls, getting dressed and nappy changes can become an Olympic sport. Rolling over is a great sign of developing knee, hip and elbow joints becoming more flexible and stronger.

Baby's Fourth Month

At this stage, the baby is much more aware of their surroundings and exploring. Play mats are a great and safe option at this stage for the baby as they may have already begun to roll over or are close to doing the same. Don't be surprised if they do it when you're not looking, so be very careful of where baby is placed. A play mat will also encourage tummy time as the baby will now be more interested in investigating objects and mirrors, which are usually attached.

> *Tip: as baby is more interested in their environment feeding can become a little tricker due to distractions around them. I used to take baby into a quieter room when possible if more people where around as I found feeding with too much going on was too difficult for baby to focus on feeding.

Feeding will be reduced at this point (I will discuss in detail in timeline breakdown). The baby's stomach will have increased in size therefore, fewer bottles with more oz's. Baby's wake windows will have also increased in length by this time. I found a sleep regression in terms of afternoon nap happened around 4months with both Anna and Molly. Don't get too disheartened as the same passed quickly (3-5 days).

Playtime will have increased with baby's wake windows (75 mins to 2.5 hours), and baby loves exploring. Give baby different materials and objects to hold (muslin cloth, blanket, rattle, ball). As I mentioned, a play mat is great as many come with different colours, shapes, and material of toys attached. Mine also had a musical animal which at this stage, the baby will love listening to. Baby will also have begun reaching out and grabbing objects and everything goes straight to baby's mouth so although exploring is exciting always supervise baby.

Continue responding to baby's 'sounds and noises'. At this age, the baby is responding and paying closer attention to your voice and facial expressions. So, repeat noises they make 'coo', 'baa', as believe it or not, this is the first step in developing their conversation skills.

Baby's Fifth Month

I'll be honest, some people love a newborn baby, I loved from month four on more. As they start to become such good fun, you start to see signs of a wee personality shining through. Now, don't get me wrong, the wee snuggle of teeny tiny is amazing, but you start to get more response from the baby and feel like they get you at this point too.

Baby may become more intent when interacting with you, listening to your every word, responding when you enter the room and when they hear your voice. They begin to show affection by hugging and holding their arms up for you to lift them. Some babies even laugh at funny noises/faces at this point. Get your phone ready for video, you will rewatch this even before month 12 is over.

Baby's ability to sit (supported) is growing at a rapid pace. If you sit your baby on the floor or your lap, they may be able to sit for a moment unaided. To help the baby in learning to sit, move her legs out in front of them, into a V-shape, this helps with their balance and reduces the risk of falling over. Again, the play mat is a great space for practising as it is soft but firm beneath them and playing with toys/teddy whilst sitting helps them develop this skill.

> *Tip: when progressing with baby's ability to sit, place larger pillows/cushions behind and to the side of baby so that you can decrease your input but also if they do fall there is a soft landing ready.

Tummy time will help the baby develop their muscles for sitting and should hopefully have become a more playful exercise for the baby. You can also help to increase a baby's leg strength by supporting them in a standing position and letting a little more weight bear on their legs while you hold them.

More baby babble and new sounds, 'blowing raspberries', 'blowing bubbles' may have begun. Continue repeating sounds back to the baby and explaining what any and all objects are around the house, out walking, and singing nursery rhymes.

Carry on with all of these as the baby is constantly developing their language and communication skills. Baby's wake window will now be between 2 to 4 hours, so conversation is a simple exercise.

Baby may begin to recognise their own name from this age, so talking directly to them and calling them by their name is important. This will encourage her language skills as she will continue to watch you intently when speaking. You may notice the baby focus on your mouth when you are talking and then try to imitate the tone of your voice. Sounds may become much more interesting at this point, so get the rattles out and see the baby smile.

Be aware of overstimulation for babies, as they are now taking in far more sights, sounds and experiences, and they can become overwhelmed. I will discuss the same in detail in the timeline breakdown regarding naptime etc. Be aware of the baby's cues for the same, their wake window will be 2 to 4 hours at this stage. So be aware of not cramming too much activity into each minute. Just exploring the house can be plenty on some days. By this stage, it will be easier to know ahead of time how the baby is feeling. As they will express emotion more clearly, e.g. cry when you leave the room, raise arms when they want to be picked up.

You will recognise when the baby needs a little more calm or quiet around them.

Baby's Sixth Month

Oh, this is fun... moving out of your room and into their own and starting solid foods. I will discuss this in detail in the timeline breakdown of how I navigated these big changes. This is an important month for the baby's development and independence.

Baby should be able to sit independently at this point, hence the weaning process. Baby can most likely roll and maybe show signs of crawling. Baby's hand control is developing, and they may begin to pass an object from one hand to the other at this stage. They will also be pulling objects towards themselves, including freshly folded laundry you've left on the sofa. Pulling and letting go of things is great fun. All this new mobility makes nappy changes and getting dressed a little trickier. I will give general tips for all in the next chapter, but be aware of where the baby is placed and never leave unattended on any raised surface! Baby's wake window at this stage will be 2.5 to 3 hours, between naps. I also found that both my girls transitioned from sleeping on their backs onto their stomachs at this point. If baby is happy sleeping on their stomach this is fine. But you may find having to re-position them until they master rolling from both front to back and back onto front.

Communication skills are developing at this point. Baby will now be able to see and hear almost as well as you. They will begin to move away from crying to communicate, and there will be an increase in babbling, using facial expressions and gestures to get your understanding. Baby may begin repeating one or two sounds, such as 'ba', 'da', 'ma'. The more you respond and repeat the baby's sounds back to them, the quicker they will learn. This includes you providing physical feedback, nodding, pointing to the objects they're interested in and telling them what they are. If the baby uses a doedee to self-soothe, now is the time to begin removing it during the day.

It was at this stage that I began removing both Anna and Molly's doedee, during the day and providing it only for nap and bedtime.

This is a great stage to begin/continue singing nursery rhymes with animal noises. Baby will be more interested in what you are saying now and will await the noises you make when pausing whilst singing. Baby's understanding of object permanence is more developed now, so watching things appear and disappear is a great game at this stage. Even simply putting a small ball under a paper cup and allowing the baby to move the cup to find the object will provide entertainment. Exploring different textiles, colours, and sounds is all great at this stage, so continue with a play mat, teddies with bells inside, colourful balls and books.

Baby's Seventh Month

Baby will hopefully have been introduced to solid foods since month six, so their use of hands and the coordination should be developing quickly at this stage. Maybe using a sippy-cup (two-handled) and may have begun clapping.

You will need to begin helping the baby to support their weight on their legs. You can do this by simply holding them on your knees and allowing weight onto their legs, you can bounce them in this position also. Baby may begin to stand whilst holding onto you or a chair for a very short period. This can also be a great age for a baby jumperoo/activity station with a seat. This is an activity device (like the activities in a play mat) but in a standing position. It has a seat to place the baby in and their feet are on the floor. You begin with very short intervals, building up on the length of time used, depending on their leg strength. This will also be a great option for keeping the baby in one place if you need to get a few practical things done.

As they are at the age of beginning to crawl, and a baby mat will no longer be a safe option to leave them in when you need to pee. Baby's wake window will be 2.5 to 3 hours still, so you will need to ensure you have safe spaces for them when you must leave the room momentarily.

Fine motor skills are also developing fast. Baby will now be able to lift small objects, pass objects from one hand to the other. Their own noise volume will increase. Banging objects on the floor is very interesting as well as their vocal reaction to completing tasks, babbling will have increased during these activities.

Baby may also begin making development towards crawling. Many babies will begin by moving from lying on their stomach to pushing up on their arms and knees, rocking back and forth. Don't be surprised if the baby initially crawls backwards, this is very common, and they soon develop leg muscles to move forward.

At this age, most babies will start teething, normally with the front two bottom teeth breaking through first. Remember, excess drool will probably be the first giveaway but be mindful that once teething has started, the baby will place all objects in their mouth to chew. So be mindful of what's in the baby's reach.

Baby's Eighth Month

Crawling and increased mobility are big milestones many babies reach this month, if they haven't already. Now is the time to attach stair gates and overall childproof your home if you haven't already. Everything is now a mobile adventure. Baby may also begin to stand whilst holding furniture or you. Ensure you are always with the baby initially standing as we have now entered the bumps and falls era. You will panic initially because suddenly, your wee baby is now mobile, it's amazing and terrifying all in one. But just breathe and enjoy their development. You won't be able to stop them from every fall or tumble, and you shouldn't anyway. This is the time for the baby to explore and develop their physical abilities, so allow them to do that under your supervision.

As with the last few months, baby will be picking up everything they come across. So, continue to be aware of what's in baby's reach and potential choking hazards within your home. Now would be the time to move any ornaments, vases, picture frames, etc. which may be within reach of the baby. Just for now, the baby is only learning how to navigate their surroundings.

Babies' communication is also rapidly developing. Baby may begin to clap their hands when happy/

excited, wave bye-bye, or even blow a kiss to familiar people. They are beginning to understand others' emotions too, and may mirror your expressions. Babies may also begin to show signs of separation anxiety at this point, where they become upset if mum/dad leaves. This is temporary and completely normal, so don't panic too much. Most will tell you just to go out the door or even go when the baby isn't looking. I did not take this approach, as disappearing did not feel right to me, therefore I always told the baby I was leaving and would be back soon. This way, the baby began to understand that when I said bye, back soon, that I would come back and like everything in my approach was the long-term. If you explain to the baby early on what things mean, chances are you won't have to suddenly introduce meaning when they're older, as they will already have the connection to what you mean and what's happening.

Baby's Ninth Month

And the introduction of "no" begins. At this stage, the baby will be exploring more than just their own toys, so you may find yourself saying "no" a lot more now. Continue to be mindful of the baby's surroundings and that you have child-proofed your home. Simple things like a cup of coffee, a glass of water, etc., being in reach of the baby can be dangerous. Baby will be reaching, grabbing, possibly furniture-walking. Furniture-walking is basically when a baby brings themselves to stand by pulling themselves up using furniture and then walking whilst holding onto the frame. A great support for babies from this age is a push-along walker, which your baby can hold onto whilst they walk. Assistance will be required in terms of steering and reversing for the foreseeable, but it is a great aid for their physical development.

> *Reminder: Don't panic about shoes as soon as baby is standing and furniture-walking. I remember everyone saying oh they need shoes as soon as they can stand up, this is not true. Babies are best left barefoot as often as possible due to the speed their feet grow and it helps to strengthen the arches of their feet and balance.

Playtime will be a lot more fun, toys with moving parts, e.g. opening doors, wheels, books with lift flaps, will all be more exciting. Baby will enjoy filling and emptying containers, e.g. balls/blocks in and out of a basket/bucket. Sorting stacks/rings is also a great toy option at this point, and rolling balls. More physically interactive toys are great for babies' current development.

Baby will be beginning to babble more clearly, hopefully even a mama or dada will have been said. To promote their communication and language development, it is advised to remove a doedee now to not affect baby's babbling or learning to talk. Continue to narrate your day to baby, "were changing your nappy", "were having pancakes and eggs for lunch". This continues to be the simplest way to promote a baby's understanding and use of language. And again, Read Read Read.

Baby's Tenth Month

At this age, most babies will be confident in crawling and continue to progress with furniture walking (cruising). Try holding both baby's hands and walking them towards you. Continue to support them using a push-along-walker and general supervision regarding their surroundings when they are standing, and walking. They will most likely fall and bump a bit more at this age, but that's part of the process. Try not to overreact when the same happens. Simply help the baby back up, if they have scared themselves, reassure the baby with a cuddle.

Some babies may begin differentiating between "mama" and "dada" and addressing both correctly. Their babbling will become more audible now and continue to support them in responding to their sounds and repeating what they may be attempting to say, e.g. "ball", "yes, that's the ball". I would also begin specifying colours at this stage, to add more words to your own vocabulary for them to hear, e.g. "this ball is blue, this ball is green". They should understand "no" and respond to their own name confidently. They may also begin to point to objects they want more purposely, a cup indicating to drink, a ball to play with, etc. As always, continue to talk, sing and read to the baby.

Baby's personality will begin to shine through now. You may notice in public settings or meeting people that they are all smiles and waving or could be a little shy and turn into you physically when unknown people address them. Don't panic too much, they are only learning and finding their own temperament. At this stage, the baby may become more interested in interacting with babies close to their age. So, continue with any baby groups/play groups you may have available within your community, or even if you have a friend or relative with young children/babies.

Baby's Eleventh Month

We are nearing the end of the baby's first year and you will not believe how quickly it went (believe me). Now, baby will be a lot more physically able, standing, squatting, holding your hand to walk (short distances). Baby will even begin to hold out their arm and/or leg when getting dressed. Baby will understand simple instructions like "no", be mindful of how often you are saying it. Try to reserve "no" for dangerous situations, otherwise you may find yourself repeating one word majority of the day. You need to allow the baby to explore.

The baby will begin to show more interest in books and pictures at this stage. Rather than feeling like you're reading aloud to yourself, the baby will most likely look and point at the pages a little more often now. If you have a library close to you, now is a great time to introduce your baby to the children's section. A lot of libraries also offer baby/toddler sessions, which you can attend free of charge.

You might start to distinguish some of a baby's babbling into words. Continue talking and repeating back to the baby to show that you are listening. This type of interaction is vital in developing a baby's understanding of two-way communication. You may notice the baby beginning to sign actions to identify a specific nursery rhyme they want to hear, e.g., opening and closing their fist for Twinkle Twinkle Little Star. Continue to ask the baby for more specific instructions, e.g. "get the ball", "pick up teddy" and see if they complete the action. Sometimes they do, sometimes they don't, but just begin to be more specific in asking the baby to complete instructions. Try to keep sentences short at this point, as they are only developing their understanding of communication. Instead of "would you like more water", simply ask "more water". At this point, it is about connecting words and understanding the meaning behind questions.

Babys Twelfth Month

My God, baby is almost one! At this stage, the baby could have already taken their first steps or be making progress towards the same. Don't panic either way, many children walk by age one, many do not. Baby should have their 1-year review with their health care professional at this stage, and any issues you have can be discussed at this time.

Playtime may increase in volume, if it hasn't already. Baby will most likely love to throw, push and knock everything down at this point. Stacking blocks and containers that baby can place other objects in and out of are more interesting now. Even just the kitchen pots and pans can be a source of entertainment now, when banged together, or provide them with a spoon to hit the pot with. They love to hear the noises they make when completing activities.

It can be common for nap and bedtime fussiness at this stage. Do not panic they have not suddenly forgotten everything you've done. Continue with your normal nap/bedtime routine, and the same will resolve quickly. I will discuss the changes made to bedtime routines throughout the timeline breakdown.

Continue talking and reading to the baby. Try and expand on describing objects, "that's the red bus", "that's the blue car". Ask the baby's opinion, "Do you want the yellow spoon or the red spoon?". Giving your baby choices will help to boost their vocabulary and knowledge of words. Similarly, when reading, ask baby to point out specific objects on the page, e.g. "where is the star?", "where is the dog?", you'll be surprised how quickly baby can correctly find what you're asking. Continue to model vocabulary and behaviours for baby, e.g. "thank you", "please", the more the baby hears words, the quicker they will use them, and it's never too early to introduce simple manners.

CHAPTER FIVE

GENERAL TIPS AND WHAT'S OFTEN OVERLOOKED

This chapter will be your shortcut to hacks. I will give a quick snapshot of tips and tricks along the way for the daily tasks, and an overview of what can sometimes be overlooked.

- **Nappy changes** – you will experience different 'issues' with nappy changes. In the beginning 'free pee' is a common one, when baby decides to urinate (or sometimes poop) mid change. So, for this, before you begin, have a new nappy open, a minimum of three wipes out of the packet, and a nappy bag open (if you're using one). For the first 6-12 weeks, you can wipe across babies' belly (just above the closed nappy) to encourage any more urine to come out before you start. I also found that if you open the nappy, allow a little air to reach the baby, this could also help any urine come out. Place a new nappy under the soiled one before you start cleaning the baby, I would also place used wipes into the soiled nappy, that way, when you're done, fold the nappy closed and place it in the bag with a new nappy already underneath, less mess. Also, for when a poonami happens, oh the joy, take baby's onesie off from top down. Roll the onesie down baby and not over their head, we don't need poop in their hair.

When the baby begins to roll and becomes more mobile, have everything ready to go. This never really changes, but they will not enjoy changing. So, if you have long hair, have it in a ponytail and swing it around above the baby's face, this is a great distraction. Give baby the wipes packet, a ball, another nappy, and/or sing. You will go through a multitude of distraction techniques, but there are a few to get you started. To be fair, you will need a few for getting the baby dressed at times too.

- **Bottles** – When the baby is distracted/not interested in feeding, I found that by taking bottle out of the mouth and replacing it with doedee for 20/30 seconds, then placing the bottle back in, helped

Molly eat more. I also (by accident) discovered Molly preferred a warmer bottle. At about 12 weeks, when trying to push the amount of oz's. I had placed Molly's bottle into a jug of hot water, when I restarted her bottle, it turned out it was the temperature that helped her to finish a bottle. Now obviously always check the temperature on your wrist, but be mindful that some babies may prefer a warmer or cooler temperature bottle.

Also be aware of the setting, baby's reach stages where they are too distracted by the environment to focus on their feed. So, if there's more noise/people than usual, try feeding in a quieter room. I found this helped with both my girls (more so around the 4-month age).

- **Time between feeds** – 2-3 hours between feeds means from starting, i.e. you started the bottle at 7 am, the next one is due at 10 am. As feeding can take 40 minutes in the beginning, I was unsure of this with Anna, but the clock starts with the beginning of the bottle, so in the early days it can feel like you are just constantly feeding the baby.

- **Medicine** – Hopefully, the baby will not require medicine too early or often, but after infant immunisations, you are advised to provide paracetamol. It is very difficult to get medicine into a baby. Try measuring the medicine in a syringe then empty contents into a bottle teat (usually size 2) and place the teat into the baby's mouth. This will help them swallow the medicine, and you will know the correct amount was administered.

- **Doedee/Pacifier** – Can be a great use when pushing time between feeds and as a general soother for the baby, especially in the early months. However, I began removing the girls doedees during the day from around 6/7 months. I did not want either of the girls to get to an age where they were asking for a doedee during the day. I began removing the doedee on walks, in the car and then just in general. I would only provide doedee for nap and bedtime by 10 months. And to be honest, with beginning to remove this aid early, there was no real issue.

- **Sleep-bag** – Place the baby into the sleep bag before the bedtime bottle. This way you do not have to get them into the sleep bag after they have had their feed and hopefully are calm and ready for sleep.

- **Shower** – I can't function without a shower in the morning, so for weeks 0-12, the baby was placed on the bathroom floor on their baby nest. Depending on the time, from 12 weeks, the baby would either be down for a morning nap already, or I would place baby into a baby chair/bouncer on the bathroom floor.

- **Weaning** – As I said, a lot of time and supervision goes into weaning in the beginning. At times, I would simply bring the baby highchair over to the sink/dishwasher/washing machine so you can get a few things done whilst they are eating.
- **Honey** – No honey before baby is 12 months, as a bacteria (Clostridium), which can cause infant botulism, can be found in honey.
- **Chores** – I would let the girls 'join me' when putting clothes wash on, loading or unloading the dishwasher, hoovering, mopping. Whatever it is, let them join (where safety allows), and both now have a clear understanding of what we're doing and want to help. Anna loves unloading the dishwasher, and both love 'sorting', aka folding (kind of) the laundry.
- **Dropping Naps** – Don't panic, most babies drop their morning nap between 10-14 months and both mine were completely different, Molly 10/11 months, Anna 14 months. I will discuss how I replaced their nap with independent play in the 9-12 months' section of the timeline breakdown.

- **Storage** – Over-the-door hang organiser, we placed one in the baby's room and the living room. It came with four pocket shelves which we divided, nappies, wipes, creams, socks, whatever you need throughout the day. It's great at saving space and having items easily accessed.
- **Nails** – Yes, your baby's little hands and feet are adorable, but their nails grow just like yours and can be a nightmare to cut. Initially, 0-6 months, we found it was easiest to use a baby nail file (electronic) during bottles. One person gave the bottle and whilst the baby was eating, another would file their nails. After 6 months, it's a little trickier and you just need to try different techniques, a toy/teddy/ball can help. It usually takes two people the first year, one to entertain the baby and one to file.
- **Teething** – Not all signs of teething are obvious. Very loose, more frequent soiled nappies, red bum can all be signs of teething. Excess drool can be helped by placing a bib under the baby's top to keep their chest dry. Can put Vaseline (a small amount) on the baby's chin to help prevent irritation to their skin.
- **Mattress Protector** – you will not regret this purchase, it will save baby blowouts and spit-up

cleaning time. I got a cot mattress protector, as I could not find one small enough for their co-sleeping crib, and simply doubled it around the crib mattress from the beginning. Once the bed sheet was secure, this saved massively from clean-up time.

- **Double up on bedtime nappy** – I found that once the girls started sleeping through the night one nappy may not hold their urine completely, leading to a lot of bedding changes. So, I found if I put 2 nappies on at night, this helped with the same. How long you may need to do this, if at all, will depend on the baby. Molly never required two nappies.

*TIP: Anna had a 'clicky hip' as a newborn, same was checked by consultant and thankfully was no issue. Some babies do have this, and an old-wife's tale was to put 2 nappies on baby to help. So, two birds one stone, I guess.

- **Batch cook** – In the first few months especially, you will have little time to eat, so batch cook what you can and freeze. Also, buy or make cereal/breakfast bars and smoothies. These are an easy go to and can be eaten/drunk one-handed.

- **Baby clothes** – Baby clothes are tiny and turn into a mess quickly. Keep onesies, baby-grows, socks, hats, tops, and bottoms in separate sections and try your best to divide clothing into age brackets from the beginning. I also found it easiest to change clothes in the baby's room in one go. So, if they're moving into 6-9 months of clothing replace all or most at the same time. It's annoying to do, but saves so much time and effort in the day-to-day. I continue to do this in Anna's room 2+ years, as it's just so much easier when getting dressed at any age.
- **9-12 month onesies** – try to get ones with grip feet. This is the stage where most babies will start standing, crawling and furniture walking, so having grips on their feet will help them. Also, if the season allows, try to get the baby barefoot as much as possible to aid with their development.
- **Quick Fix** – If you or your baby is restless or agitated, get outside or into water, This is one of the simplest and quickest fixes I have found for both.
- **Floor time** – Is the simplest activity you can do for a baby in their first year, but also when they are a toddler. Many overlook simply interacting with their child. Floor time (not tummy time) can begin

when the baby is around 2-3 months old, depending on their wake windows and interest. Floor time can be both independent, where you are nearby but not beside the baby, and interactive when you are actively involved with the baby's activities. Studies have shown that floor time supports a baby's cognitive and physical development, as it provides opportunities for free play. Floor time will support baby's motor skills as when baby is young, most of the time they are 'contained' either in your arms, pram, swaddle, etc. Floor time allows baby to use their big muscles, which eventually leads to rolling, crawling and walking. It is also a way for you and your baby to bond.

Floor time will change with the baby's age. Initially you will need to stay close to the baby, provide appropriate toys, materials and alter the baby's lying positions. But this will change as the baby grows, supporting them to roll over, sit independently, etc. Floor time doesn't need to be complicated. You can simply lie beside the baby and sing, show them books, give them different materials to touch, e.g. a scarf, a sock, a towel. This is again where a play mat comes in handy, as baby can play securely and build on their ability to play independently.

Floor time will become 1:1 play as the baby grows, which is great for strengthening your bond but also supporting their development. Ensure you mix independent and interactive floor time as this allows baby to build their self-confidence, but also reassures them that you are with them.

- **Overstimulation** – This one really surprised me, in that I seemed to be the only person aware of how easily a baby becomes overstimulated. Everything is new to a baby, and I remember speaking to other mums who would talk about the baby not settling, sleeping, or finishing a bottle, but never taking into consideration the environments they were expecting the baby to carry out these tasks. Or the activities carried out prior to 'naptime' with no wind down, and then being surprised that the baby doesn't sleep.

If you organise a schedule, you are more than likely aware of overstimulating baby, but be mindful of this on-going. At different stages in a baby's first year, distractions, milestones, growth spurts etc., will affect a baby's ability to manage stimulation.

Be aware of how you fill babies' time prior to nap and bedtime. You don't need to always entertain the baby, allow them to amuse themselves (with you alongside obviously) once they are capable. Do not have screens, music on continuously and if you do, be aware of what you are watching and/or listening to. It sounds like overkill, I know, but you need to be mindful of how much chaos is happening around baby because in the initial stages, everything is chaos. They don't know the world or what's going on in it, so be aware of what and how much you are exposing them to.

CHAPTER SIX

TIMELINE BREAKDOWN

Throughout each of the following sections, I will discuss and explain how I implemented a feeding and sleep schedule. The daily routine I took with both girls and the practical support I implemented for the baby's development. The schedule I ultimately finished with is still running today. Some elements change with age, e.g. the method of feeding, the routine of bedtime expands. But the timing of the schedule stays the same, give or take 15 minutes. This is what worked for me. Obviously, adapt times as needed for your lifestyle, but the methods of establishing it will remain the same. Everything I did was with the aim of long-term goals, not short-term fixes. Which takes consistency initially, but believe me, it pays off in the long run. Before 6 months, both Anna and Molly knew their routine and thrived.

Baby's First Year of Life

Before we begin, I remember reading somewhere, *'you never know the last time you do something with your child will be the last time'*, so I want to share the first time this reality hit me. From Anna was a few weeks old, she would come upstairs with me every evening to get ready for bed, get me ready, not her. This was when I would clean my face and get into my pyjamas before starting her bedtime routine. I told her that it was 'lotions and potions time'. It began with her lying on her baby nest on the bathroom floor, then sitting in her bouncer, to having her walk about with her own toiletry bag (of my empty moisturisers and deodorant bottles). By about 14 months old, Anna would walk towards the stairgate every evening and say 'loish and poish mamma'. We did this every night, until one evening when she was about 19/20 months old, she simply didn't say it and we have never done it since. I remember this so clearly as it was the first 'decision' Anna made regarding her routine. It wasn't a change we made regarding her development or age, it was a choice she made that she didn't need it in her routine anymore. This was the first time I realised you really don't know when the last time you do something with your child, is the last time.

So even on your hardest day, for whatever reason that may be, take a breath, look at their little face and remember how lucky you are that they chose you. Time goes so fast; everyone tells us, but just wait until one day the reality of time hits you.

O – 6 Weeks

During this period, you cannot and will not establish anything close to a routine there is no point in saying otherwise. You have a newborn baby, your tiny little human will decide when they eat, when they sleep and anything else for that matter. These first few weeks are for nothing other than loving and getting to know your little person and your own recovery. Regardless of your birthing experience we all need recovery time. Which is a lot easier if this baby is your first but take every opportunity to rest. If your partner, family member or friend offers to watch baby so you can eat, take baby for a walk so you can sleep, say yes. Mum guilt will naturally kick in, ignore it. Don't worry about routines this early, some will say you can and should begin a routine with the baby as soon as you get home. I chose to take the first six weeks to recover and get to know my baby. Which I felt strengthened, my ability to decide on a routine and implement it once we got to week 6. For now, just enjoy the baby scrunch (take a video, I never did, and it kills me now). Their little milk-drunk face, the startle reflex (cuteness overload) and falling asleep mid-bottle.

What you may be able to discern during this time is their different cries. There has been specific research done regarding babies' cries and universal findings that there are specifically five types of cries. By noticing the difference between your baby's cries, it will help you tremendously when trying to establish a routine. As it will help you figure out what your baby is trying to tell you. Knowing the difference in cries is also a massive help further down the line when figuring out why the baby is waking at night, if not hungry. It sounds complicated, but you will develop your ability to decode your baby's cries quite naturally and it gets easier as you get to know your little one.

The five crying sounds

- **Hunger**: 'Neh'. Beginning with a long, low-pitched cry that is repetitive. If not noticed quickly, the same will become longer and louder with short pauses. Other signs of hunger include smacking lips, clenched fists, and putting their hands to their mouth.

  What can help: Simple, feed the baby.

- **Upper Wind (burp)**: 'Eh'. This 'eh' sound is a clear indication of trapped wind; the sound is made by a baby when trying to push air out from their chest.

    What can help: Burp baby, try different burping positions. When burping a baby, your hand movement should be primarily upward on their back like you're trying to push air up. This one is easier to prevent over time once you understand which winding positions work best for the baby, but also the speed of feeding.

- **Lower wind/Gas:** 'Eairh or earggghh'. Sounds like a long 'Air' sound and usually starts with an open mouth, tongue held back, and a taut belly, signalling lower discomfort in the abdomen.

    What can help: Massage the baby belly or feet to quickly relieve any digestive discomfort. Wiggle and stretch the baby's hips to help relieve discomfort.

- **Discomfort**: 'Heh'. It can be caused by being too hot or cold, a wet or soiled nappy, or overstimulation. It is a mild cry, on and off, that again increases if not recognised quickly.

    What can help: Check the nappy and baby's temperature (placing your hand on the baby's chest is a simple way of checking temperature, or place your fingers on the back of the baby's neck). If both are fine, try holding the baby for a little comfort.

- **Tired**: 'Owh, or oah'. A whiny, nasal and continuous cry that builds in intensity. Other signs include yawning, zoning out/staring off into space and/or eye-rubs or ear-tugs.

    What can help: If you are not able to put the baby into their crib, try finding a quieter, darker room if in someone else's home. If you are out and about, try rocking the baby back and forth in their stroller or your arms.

The Pain Cry, although not in the universal list, you will know this cry when you hear it, and it is awful and scary. It is high-pitched and piercing, your baby will make an 'eairh' sound and is easy to distinguish due to the level of urgency and distress. I remember the first time Anna cried the pain cry, your heart stops. This was the first sign of her silent reflux. There can be many reasons for the pain cry, most common are gas, constipation, colic, reflux and teething.

There are video resources available online to enable you to hear these cries and help you navigate your own baby's cry/sounds.

The Witching Hour

This is completely normal and usually begins once the baby reaches 2-3 weeks of age. Now, most babies will experience this early evening, 5-11pm. Baby will become fussy, and intense crying usually follows. Like everything, all children are different, some may cry for one hour, others may cry for multiple. I found the timing of the 'witching hour' to be different with both Anna and Molly. Anna was early evening, 5-7 pm, and Molly was 12-2pm. This period can last until the baby is 12 weeks(ish). However, I didn't find that either of my girls experienced it consistently each night and for more than 2-3 weeks. There are varied reasons for this period, and I will tell you what I found worked best for getting the girls through the same.

Reasons for the 'witching hour'

- **Overstimulation** – I have discussed this in most sections, and that I was much more focused on being aware of overstimulation than any of my 'mom friends' seemed to be. Babies are brand new, every sound, smell, touch, and experience is new and unknown to them, so obviously this can agitate them.

During 0-6 weeks from 4pm, I would have tried to minimise noise within the house. No TV, no music, and limit visitors, if any, to try and help with this.

- **A Growth Spurt** – this will happen throughout the baby's first year and can cause the baby to be hungrier and perhaps more unsettled than usual.
- **Fatigue** – in the same way as we can all get close to the end of the day, a baby can simply be ready for whined down.

Tips to get through

- **Movement** – I found with both my girls that a baby carrier was great during the 'witching hour'. Whether it was the swaying of walking around or the close contact, both were soothed when in the carrier.
- **Quiet** – Try to eliminate as much disturbance/ noise as you can. I would try not to be out and about during this period once I knew when they were likely to experience the witching hour. I would try to avoid visiting people, popping out

for groceries, coffee (not that I was wanting to do any of these things 2 weeks in) and TV/music switched off.

- **Doedee** – This is when a doedee was introduced with both Anna and Molly, as it comforted both, and I was okay with that.
- **Head for a walk** – I always found a walk in the pram comforted both girls (at any age). Even better if you have a partner/family member who can take the baby for a quick walk. In the early days you are exhausted, so if you have this option, take it. But if you don't, you will always benefit from getting outside. Even on my most tired days, when I really didn't think I had the energy, after the first five steps, the rejuvenation that comes from getting out.
- **Darkness** – What I found settled Molly more during the witching hour was bringing her to a quiet, darker room. I would take her upstairs, close the blinds and simply walk around the room with her, which calmed her.

This period is short-lived, and the length of the 'hour' is different for all babies. As I said, it is not always the evening, and it is not always an hour. I didn't find that either Anna or Molly had the same time every day/night, and it wasn't every consecutive night either. You will be okay, and you will get through this. I think, because it is so early in the baby's journey that it can take more out of you than you expect. But like everything, it will soon be a distant memory.

Distinguish Night and Day

I remember friends/family members saying to me 'just hope they know night from day'. Research shows newborn baby (0-8 weeks) commonly confuse night and day. It is a common occurrence and stems from babies' underdeveloped circadian rhythm. Neither of my girls confused night and day, and I will tell you what I did to prevent this.

- **Take naps in the open (bright)** – although dark and quiet is best for the baby to sleep, during this period, I was more interested in distinguishing night from day. Research suggests that having the baby nap where it is bright and noisy will help them recognise the difference between day and night. You may also avoid swaddling or using a sleep bag for naps these initial few weeks, reserving it for bedtime.
- **Lift a sleeping baby** – I remember everyone saying, 'do not lift a sleeping baby', well, I did.

Once Anna or Molly napped longer than 2 hours, I would lift them. This helped them get more wake time and learn that nighttime is for practising their longer sleep stretches. Wake windows at this age are minimal to begin with (45-60 mins), look out for your baby's tired cues and you will recognise quicker when they need to nap/sleep.

Early tired cues include:
- Zoning out/staring off into space
- Rubbing eyes/nose
- Less social/more clingy
- Red brows/eyes
- Pulling ears

- **Feed baby every 2-3 hours** – In the beginning, it can be more difficult to stretch the time between feeds. But you can try to feed baby every two to three hours. I lifted both girls if they were sleeping when their feed was due, and I'll let you know that nothing dramatic happened, they ate.

- **Include a bedtime routine** – I will discuss this in depth in the next timeline breakdown, as I began a bedtime routine with both Anna and Molly once they were 6 weeks old. Research shows that having a bedtime routine before putting the baby down each night has been proven to result in more sound sleepers who sleep for longer periods at night. Some advise starting a routine from the day you get home. I'll be honest, at this stage, the feeds were too irregular, and I was too tired, but you can begin from Day 1.

6 – 12 weeks

The difference between week 6 and week 12 is monumental. Your focus during these six weeks is to introduce a routine. Begin with choosing a morning wake-up time, aim for three hours between feeds and begin a bedtime routine you will be happy to repeat for 6-9 months. I want you to really think about the times you are aiming to set for wake time, lunchtime, bedtime, etc. As give or take 20 minutes, my girls still eat and sleep within the same schedule 2+ years later.

There will be times during the 6-12week window when everything you are trying to do seems pointless and that nothing is falling into place. But you need to stick with it, stay consistent in your approach, and it will pay off tenfold. It will seem both ridiculous and impossible, but from the age of 6 weeks, I began lifting both girls for their morning feed at 7 am and tried to stretch the time between bottles to three hours. I would put them down for a nap and introduce a bedtime routine from 6 weeks. Baby may still nap at other stages of the day, e.g. out for a walk, when in the car, but I set the morning and afternoon nap in place from 6 weeks. Where you are purposeful and consistent with the time and routine of both their am and pm nap. It will seem pointless when you begin, but believe me, it works. By 9 weeks Anna slept through the night, and Molly slept through the night at 11 weeks.

Throughout weeks 6-12, you will be aiming to increase the amount of baby food intake (oz's) during the day, in fewer bottles. So, you will be pushing time between feeds to 3 hours whilst introducing a wake-up, nap and bedtime throughout 6-12 weeks. By week 12, the length of time it takes to feed the baby will most likely have gone from 40 minutes to less than 20 minutes. Their wake windows have lengthened, meaning you're planning more outings and activities to fill the day, and hopefully, nap and bedtime are set (almost).

This is the beginning of introducing all things routine. Research continues to show the benefits of a routine for babies and children. When babies have a consistent routine, it provides a sense of security, supports their development and the bond between child and parent. Routine to some seems like a forced timeframe, when in fact we all function within a routine daily, it's the way we work. For a baby, this consistency helps them to understand what to expect each day. Who the important people in their life are, and ultimately, the security created through a routine is the foundation for bonding and thriving in early childhood.

I believe that eating and sleeping go hand in hand. Until you get feeds organised, you cannot progress with sleep patterns, so start with the baby's feeding schedule. There will be a natural 'window' between feeds. As your baby grows, they should begin taking larger feeds therefore, you should get more time between bottles naturally. I aimed for bottle feeds to be 7am, 10am, 1pm, 4pm, 7pm. In the early stages (6-8 weeks), I would offer a 'dream feed' around 9:30/10 pm, just as they were so small. However, the last bottle soon became the 7pm feed, and I will discuss the transition of this. Also, pay attention to your baby, neither of my girls went three hours between each bottle, and that's okay. The 1 pm quickly became the 12:30pm, the 4pm was closer to 3:30pm, and that's fine, you don't need to be exact every time. Obviously change feeding times according to your lifestyle.

From 6 weeks old, I started trying to get as much of the bottle into the girls. Anna would finish 99%

of bottles, to the extent she would need to suck until she heard it was empty. With Molly, it was a different story, until she was about 6 months old, getting a full bottle into Molly was a mission. Now I'm not saying to force a bottle into the baby's mouth, but Molly would need help not losing interest. Remember a toddler running around is very interesting when you're 2 months old. You can use a damp cloth, cotton ball and just stroke their cheek, tickle their feet to help them eat more. I also found with Molly that if I gave her a doedee for less than a minute, then quickly removed the doedee and replaced it with the bottle, she would eat more. Molly never really finished a bottle until she was 6months old, so you'll know when to accept the lost oz's.

As well as increasing the amount in bottles at this stage, it is also the time to try and push the time between each feed. I would try to push for 3-hour feeds. With some bottles, this is easier than others. As I mentioned, neither of my girls had their 'lunchtime bottle' at 1pm, both would rather be sleeping at this stage, so their bottle moved to 12:30pm. The simplest way I found to stretch time between bottles was to know your baby's cry. By 6 weeks you should be pretty accurate in distinguishing the baby's different cries. Which will help you in stretching the time between bottles as you will know other avenues to explore before offering a feed. Thankfully, baby's hunger cry will most likely be the first you understand, it's the most obvious of the cries. After 6 weeks, you cannot continue to feed the baby any and every time they cry, as they will only ever snack, and a routine will never be established. So, to begin pushing time between feeds, get out of the house. Go for a walk, drive, attend a class, visit family/friends, even if it's only for 30/60 minutes. I found that by getting out and doing something, it was easier to stretch the time between feeds to 3 hours. If you don't have the energy to get out, walk around your house holding/wearing the baby and talk. Even just telling the baby what's in each room will pass the time and, in most circumstances, 'entertain' the baby long enough to push the next feed. It was also at this stage I found offering the girls a doedee helped to soothe them when pushing bottles. I found there were maybe two bottles out of the five which were harder to push, which is fine. If I got to 2.5 hours that was close enough, but try your best to get three bottles to 3-hour windows.

At 6 weeks, I would begin lifting both girls at 7 am for their morning feed. Now let me be clear, in the beginning, both girls may have had a bottle feed at 5:30am, but I would still lift them at 7am. Any earlier feed was done as a night feed (in the dark, no talking, etc.). I would, where possible, have the bottle made before lifting the baby. So, I would open the curtains, say 'good morning', lift the baby from their cot and change their nappy. I did not change their clothes at this point, that's up to you. I would put music on quietly in the background. I would then begin the bottle, talking throughout to distinguish the difference between a night feed and the "we are getting up to start the day" feed. I would then burp the baby following which I would have a coffee that I had brought up in an insulated cup before lifting the baby. So, I would place the baby on my bent legs facing me and talk while I drank the sweet nectar that is caffeine. With Molly (baby no. 2), her morning routine began the same way, only I would have taken her downstairs to have her bottle. As following her first feed, I would be lifting Anna, so it was just easier at this stage to already have Molly downstairs. I would then either put the baby on the bed for tummy time or just to relax. Then, I had their 'baby nest' ready to place them on the bathroom floor while I had a shower. Enjoy the ability to do this because once they start rolling, a different set-up of equipment will be required. Anna liked the bathroom, Molly not so much. Molly preferred to go for her morning nap around 8:45/9:00, Anna was always closer to 09:30. So again, you will soon figure out your own baby's wake windows.

Before putting the baby down for their morning nap, I would change their nappy/clothes, tell them "time for a wee snooze, mummy's got to get dressed", place them into their crib and leave. If the baby cried, I would return, place my hand on their stomach and repeat "time for a wee snooze", count to 100, then leave. Most of the time, I found the morning nap the easiest, with little reassurance/settling required. I didn't pull curtains during the day until the baby was 6 months. I would play white noise on their sound machine teddy (20 minute timer) and leave the room. In general, if further reassurance/settling was required, whether it be at naptime or bedtime, I would repeat the same steps, leaving more time between returning to the room. So, first cry, go in immediately, second cry wait one minute, third cry wait 2 minutes, etc. I would never have left the baby to cry longer than 5 minutes continuously, but honestly, it never really happened. Usually, the morning nap is relatively short (30 mins), so majority of the time I would just get dressed and have a coffee. When the baby woke, I would bring them downstairs. Depending on the time (how close to 10 am), I would either do the next feed or read/floor time/tummy time. Just to note if the baby did not wake by 10 am. I would lift them for their feed. Once the second feed was done, I would normally have gone out for a walk/attend a class, etc. I don't know why, but I always found getting out of the house easier in the morning. Probably because you have a little more energy in the morning. I found it gave me a bit of a lift for the rest of the day.

The afternoon feed, was due 1pm however, I found neither of my girls would stretch to that, so 12:30pm it was. Following which I would put them down for their nap at 1pm to 1:15pm (again, remember feeding time will shorten between 6 and 12 weeks. Week 6 baby may have gone down closer to 1:30, week 12, 1pm).

Now, the afternoon nap, I found a little trickier and it depends on the baby's wake windows. I found with both girls that four hours between naps and going to bed was enough. There will be times, e.g. growth spurt/teething/sickness, when the baby will require more or less sleep, which is grand. I am talking about sleep on the average day. The afternoon nap, I found I needed to be more tuned in to both girls' sleep cues. Miss them or leave it too long between noticing a sleep cue and heading for their crib, would be the difference in settling very quickly for a nap or spending 40 mins trying to get them to fall asleep.

Afternoon nap, same as the morning nap; I would not pull curtains or play music, I would change the baby's nappy, tell them "nap time", put them into their crib and switch on their white noise to play for 20 minutes. I took the same approach with all nap/sleep times, place a hand on their stomach, count to 100, then leave. The same approach to any settling that was required. As I said at the beginning, my approach is not complicated, but it is consistent. I'll be honest, I usually had a nap at the same time however, I would try to allow the baby to fall asleep before I would lie down. So, given that until 6 months of age they slept in my bedroom, I would go get something to eat, and hopefully 10 or so minutes later they would be asleep, and I would then get into bed.

Now the other thing you will need to begin doing from now is to limit baby's naptime. If baby goes down at 1pm, they are back up at 3pm. The reason for this is so they are not asleep too close to bedtime. The general thinking is for the baby to be awake no less than 4 hours before bed. So up from nap at 3pm, going down for bedtime 7/7:30pm. Plus, they will be due a feed at 3:30/4pm. I know there will be days when you really, really don't want to lift the baby, but at this early stage, you are trying to get them into a routine. So for now, you need to be as precise with feed and sleep times. There will be a little more give and take a few months down the line, but for now, you're going to have to lift them.

Following their nap, they will have another feed, after which floor-time/wear baby/walk is an option. I was always mindful of creating a period of evening wind down within the house from about 5/5:30pm. Being mindful that I was introducing a bedtime and routine, I wanted to help the baby as much as possible. So, at 5:30pm, the house would be quiet, no screens, or music would be on in the background. Soft lighting where possible and limiting visitors where possible. Again, this may seem drastic, but it's just at this early stage you want to aid the baby's understanding as much as you can. I would set up the baby's bedtime prior to bringing them to bed (outlined in Chapter 3: Sleeping). I found at this age that one of two options worked best. It was either easier to have the sleep bag open and placed in the baby's cot for them to be placed into after burping, or for the baby to be wearing their sleep bag during the bedtime feed. However, when wearing it, you run the risk of spit up, etc. and the sleep bag needing to be changed before bed. Following their last bottle repeat settling steps as required. I would not have introduced music at this stage, but simply just switched their white noise/ heartbeat on for twenty minutes and night light on timer.

Now there are nights when this will work seamlessly, other nights more bottle is needed (usually

2-3 oz). You may need to return after leaving to settle baby anything from 3 to 7 times to repeat "sleep-time" settling routine. Other nights where you barely get out of the room for 2 minutes without having to repeat the settling routine. But as I have said, 'long-term' goals. I did not aim for either of the girls to be asleep when I put them down at night. I helped them settle to put themselves to sleep. I did not rock, ssh, or sing my babies to sleep. Obviously, when sick/teething, you will do whatever is required to comfort and soothe the baby. I am talking average nighttime, which has saved me and them tenfold in the long run. My aim was for the baby to be happy going into bed and not require a 'nighttime ritual' every night.

Initially, at 6 weeks I would offer baby a 'dream feed' at about 9:30/10pm. However, I found majority of the time neither would really eat much of this bottle maybe 2 oz's. So after about a week I stopped offering the dream feed and just waited for baby to naturally wake for another feed. By 8 weeks, Anna had only one night feed around 2 am, and Molly at 2 am and 5:30 am. By 9 weeks, Anna had dropped all night feeds, and Molly by 11 weeks. I found that the girls naturally dropped the early morning 2 am feed, and it was more pushing Molly's 5:30 am until 7 am. Both would wake around 5:30/6 am between 6-9 weeks, so it was more a case of ensuring to decode their cry. Try and soothe them with doedee, hand on stomach, stroke their face. Trying other options before lifting baby for a bottle to try and push them closer to a 7 am wake-up feed. As I've said previously, you will know the baby's hunger cry and you will know when a feed is required. At this stage it is about not jumping straight to offering a feed and maybe just a little reassurance/comfort for the baby. Between 8-9 weeks, Anna just woke closer and closer to 7 am, Molly the same between 9-11weeks. As I said, nothing complicated is required in my approach, but you do need to pay attention to the baby's cues and stay consistent in your approach.

3 – 6 months

*Personal request: For the love of humankind, this is when you stop referring to your child's age in weeks. Your child is not 22 weeks, they are 5 months.

*Reminder – go up a bottle teat size.

I always remember Anna's health visitor saying to me that there is a natural 'settling period' for babies between 12-14 weeks, and it was true with both my girls. If you have still been struggling to push time between bottles, finish feeds or figure out wake windows, now is the stage where you should hopefully see a natural settling of your baby's routine. There is nothing new being introduced to the baby's routine at this stage. Continue with nap, feeding and sleep schedule as the previous 6 weeks. Things should begin to cement a bit more now, if they haven't already done so. Some parents push for four-hour windows between feeds at this stage. However, as both my girls were sleeping through the night, I did not push for the same. The choice is yours, and if you do want to try for 4-hour windows simply just repeat the same steps as before.

Our Routine at this age:

07:00: Wake time and first feed.

07:30-08:30: Coffee/breakfast, tummy/floor time, shower, get baby dressed and a new nappy.

First Nap: 09:00 Molly. Anna, 09:30. I would get dressed and have a coffee during nap.

10:00: Second feed

10:30/10:45: Get out of the house, whether it was for a walk, class, or visiting friends/family.

12:30/12:45: Home and Lunchtime bottle

13:00/13:15: Afternoon nap– we <u>all</u> napped.

15:00/15:15: Wake up from nap (exactly two hours from the time they went down for nap

15:30/15:45: Fourth feed

16:30-18:00: Chores while baby wearing, floor-time/play mat/books and sometimes another walk. All electronics are off throughout the house.

18:00-18:30: Whine down before bedtime routine. I would complete my bedtime routine 'loish and poish', i.e. clean my face, get jammies on. Set up their bedtime so night-light on instead of main bedroom light. Instrumental music on low, nappy and baby-grow, onsie, sleep bag all laid out and ready to go.

18:30: I would bring the baby upstairs to get ready for bed, change their clothes and nappy, talking softly, reminding them throughout that it's bedtime. Can complete baby massage, sing, or read to the baby.

18:55: Placed into their next to me cot. End of talking.

19:00: Return to complete the last feed. Set night-light on 1-hour timer.

19:30: Baby placed into next-to-me for the night, white noise set for 20minutes. Place your hand on the baby's stomach, count to 100 and leave.

What I did find with Molly between 3 and 4 months was that she wanted her 'bedtime bottle' earlier. Molly became more tired and agitated waiting for her last bottle at 7pm. So, we ended up moving it earlier to 6:40pm, and she would be in bed at about 7pm. This may have been due to just having more activity going on in the house, as Anna was running around in full toddler mode, or simply Molly's temperament. I remember worrying about how early her last bottle was, but she was happier. And having the 6:40pm bedtime bottle made no difference to her wake-up time in the morning. So as always, aim for what schedule you want but leave room to respond to baby's cues.

By 3 months, you should now be starting to see your way through the newborn haze. Feedings should be a lot quicker now; nap and sleep time should hopefully be on a schedule, and you feel less rushed to get everything done during the day. It should be easier now to arrange outings, catch-ups and activities outside of your home (if that's what you wish). Everyone's different, some people are straight back to hairdresser appointments, coffee catch-ups, baby yoga/sensory classes from week 2. Don't be pressured by other people's social media perceptions to feel that you need to be doing more. Do what you are comfortable and capable of doing. If you choose two mornings each week to plan an activity, that's brilliant, if you choose five, well check you out. But make the decision for you and your baby, not what you think you should be doing. Also, make sure you research local community sources for activities. Most libraries offer free rhythm and rhyme classes, and community centres can offer sensory/yoga classes. Don't always feel the need to pay for every course/class. Research what may be available for you and your baby within your community. The first person to ask would be your health visitor, as they are a great source of local information.

With that said, I feel there is such pressure put on mothers to provide ongoing resources of entertainment and activities for babies and throughout toddlerhood. I will discuss the opportunity of self-play and allowing your baby to be bored in the later months. Today's society is so focused on always having something going on, something to do. Never enabling a child to sit in silence, aka boredom. I will discuss this further and the choices I made in allowing my children to amuse themselves once they are a little older but keep this in mind even at this very young age. Baby does not always need to be the centre of what's happening. Yes, they will be with you at all stages throughout what you need to do (groceries, housekeeping, etc.), but don't fall into constantly entertaining them from the beginning, as you are only setting yourself up for the future. Long-term goals over short-term fixes, remember.

As I said, by now it may seem like you have a lot of time back during the day, and baby's wake windows will most likely have increased anywhere from 75 mins to 2.5 hours. Therefore, we need ideas to support baby's development. Don't panic, as I mentioned above, of course look at classes, but you can do plenty at home, at little to no cost to support your baby's development. Playtime at 3 months old can be as simple as reading (which I advised to do from the beginning anyway). Baby will most likely be starting to reach to try and grab objects, you can support this by providing different textures/materials to grab as well as toys. Try scarves, towels, blankets, ribbons, bubble wrap, anything and everything will help baby's hand-eye coordination. Let them reach for the materials and play with them in their hands. You can also attach ribbon/paper strands onto the baby's mobile or play mat (overhead frame) so they can lie down and play independently (under supervision). A baby mirror is also a great source of entertainment at this age. Most play mats come with one attached, or you can buy individual mirrors.

At 4 months tummy time should be advancing. Most baby's will roll at 4 months and to encourage the same, you can try placing toys just out of the baby's reach when they are on their tummy to encourage them to reach and roll to a different position. Again, the baby mirror is great for encouraging more movement during tummy time and toys placed above the baby on their play mat.

It is common for babies to have a sleep regression at 4 months. This is when a previous nap or bedtime can be disrupted from their routine. It is said to be due to the baby's brain development. Signs of sleep regression are usually frequent wakings, difficulty falling asleep, irritability and reduced sleep duration. I found with both girls that any sleep regressions they experienced affected their naptimes rather than bedtime, and thankfully only lasted 3-5 days. When the baby is experiencing a sleep regression stick with your previous routine. The routine you have been setting from week 6 (or before) will continue to help baby establish day and night routines. Which should aid baby during a sleep regression as you continue to repeat the previous routine. As I said, I found that both girls' afternoon nap was disrupted at 4 months, but I continued as normal at naptime. I brought the baby upstairs, got them changed into a new nappy, new onesie and down for a nap in their sleep bag. For a few days, the baby may have babbled for 40 minutes before going to sleep. Or the baby may have cried for 20 minutes, babbled 20 minutes and then no sleep was had. But continue to carry out their normal routine, still put the baby down for a nap. Lie beside them and continue to say, "nap time", and hopefully the regression will be over as quickly as it began. There is nothing specific you can do to speed up sleep regressions or prevent them from happening. But if you have been consistent with the baby's routine until now, they should cope a little easier with sleep regressions and fall back into their usual routine quickly. As with everything in my approach, repetition and consistency.

Reread Chapter 4 – Milestones. Just a reminder that the baby's development at this stage is much more intent on interacting with you. Showing affection and responding to their name between five and six months. So, continue to speak directly to the baby, read books and explain what anything and everything is on walks, in the house, etc. Baby will be more likely to become overstimulated at this stage due to longer wake windows (2-4 hours). But it will be easier for you to navigate baby's emotions at this point. A big physical milestone they will be working towards is sitting unaided. Support their development by supporting them to sit for short periods, building up to sitting unsupported. When allowing the baby to sit unaided, place cushions around the baby to fall onto.

At month 5, you will most likely be thinking of moving the baby into their own room. From this stage, I began introducing the baby's room a little more during the day. Now, some of you may have had your baby's nursery ready before they arrived, but I did not. We got Anna's room ready when she was about 5months old, and Molly's about the week she turned 6 months (poor second child). Whenever you have the baby's room ready, introduce them to the room. Maybe have a bottle feed once a day and have tummy time a few times a week in their room so that they become familiar with the new environment. I also began putting the baby into the cot bed in their new room for naptime the week of them turning 6 months. This was to introduce the new sleep setting to them in a small way before the 'big move' to their own room. As well as this, I began spending time in their room after their 4pm bottle to again just introduce the room to the baby. Simply bring a toy/teddy/book in and just spend twenty minutes in their room and allow them to become more aware of their surroundings. All of which should aid them when it comes to moving from your bedroom to their own room.

In preparation for the 'big move', you will need to get their room ready. Don't get carried away with accessories, toys and colours. This can all come once you have an older child, but right now, the baby's room needs to be calm and neutral in most aspects. The essentials you will need are a cot-bed, we went for one which could then change into a toddler bed. You will need to get mesh railing covers for the baby at this age also to prevent them from getting their legs or arms caught between the railings. Bonus, it also helps to contain doedees through the night. Chest of drawers/tall boy, which had a fitted changing table on the top, which could later be removed. Wardrobe and another of the over-the-door hanging shelves for storage, night light and Alexa. We chose pastel colours throughout the room, any pictures/stencils on the wall were all neutral colours.

We chose to move the baby into their own room at six months due to safety concerns of SIDS decreasing by this age. Also following 6 months of age, the baby will become more aware of their sleeping environment, who shares the room and which room they are in. Therefore, we were comfortable moving the baby into their own room at this age to aid the process. Also, neither could continue to fit in their next-to-me and needed a cot-bed at this stage. I will discuss the process of moving in the next section.

At this stage, you will also want to decide on how you are going to approach the weaning process. Get the highchair out from storage and order the full-body bibs.

6 – 9 months

Reminder – go up a bottle teat size.

Oh, month six… this is a huge turning point for you and baby. I remember thinking that feedings, nap and bedtime, where all running smoothly, and now, I must wean and move the baby into their own room. It is scary regardless of whether this is the first baby or not. Just breathe and remember this is an important period for the baby's development and independence. There are a lot of changes I made in this three-month window to aid the baby's development. I will discuss all in detail, but just to give you an idea, the baby will be a lot more mobile during this time. Beginning with sitting, then crawling, and most likely standing (aided). You will need to consider adaptations to your daily routine to support all of this.

From 6 months of age, I began removing baby's doedee more and more throughout the day. This was to avoid further difficulty removing the doedee once the baby had become dependent on it. I started by removing the doedee during walks in the pram and car journeys. Working up to simply leaving the doedee in their bedroom after naptime and morning wake up by 8 months old. I found by doing this early with both girls, there were no real issues or upset caused. They were young enough to build the association of having a doedee only when they were sleeping.

Another skill I worked on supporting was independent self-play. Now supervision will remain constant for some time yet, but I promoted independent play where possible. For example, now that the baby can sit independently, I would place them into their cot with a book, teddy or toy for just five to ten minutes while I cleaned their room or put clothes away. Over time, building up to leaving them within their cot while I went into the next room, etc. This was in preparation for the day that their morning nap was dropped. So that they would be able to play within their own space while I could still go and get showered and dressed alone. I will discuss this transition in the 9-12 months section.

Similarly, a jumperoo is a great tool at this point. As I said, the baby will be much more mobile and moving around freely within this three-month window, as crawling will happen. So, when it comes to mopping floors, putting clothes on the line, you will need to think of new ways to safely contain the baby when you need to be hands-free. A jumperoo is great for developing their physical abilities and their self-play. Beginning with short periods of time, five or ten minutes, I would place the baby into the jumperoo, go make a coffee and return to sit with them in the jumperoo. This will help the baby's development and independence from always needing you for entertainment. Another great option is a play pen; I'll give you a tip a travel cot is a fantastic option for the same. Most likely, your house will be coming down with all things baby equipment, toys and appliances. I did not want a huge play pen taking up more floor space, but I also knew I wouldn't use it that often. From 6 months, I set up a travel cot in the kitchen for the baby to use as a play pen, again supporting independent play. I found this worked great when I needed to get practical tasks (mop the floor, especially) done.

From 6 months, I was also conscious of my response time to the baby waking and crying out. It may sound harsh, but calm down, I simply mean that once the baby was happy in their routine (from 3 months), I became a little more aware of leaving time between the baby waking up and me going in to get them. This was because you will not always be able to go straight into the baby once they wake for any number of reasons. I wanted to get the baby comfortable with waiting. I just started leaving a minute to five before going into the baby, and I found that they would begin babbling, moving around, and no issues arose. I think we are made to feel like a baby is not capable of being alone, and we need to attend to them immediately, when this just isn't true. Let the baby be comfortable in their own company and just see the difference this has once they become a toddler. If Anna wakes before 07:30 in the morning now at 2 years old, she will simply get out of bed, get a book, teddy or her Toni Box and talk away to herself for twenty/thirty minutes before looking for me. I genuinely believe this is because she knows she is cared for. She knows someone will be in soon, and that she is happy to amuse herself in the safe environment she knows she lives in. As I continue to say, start with long-term goals over short term fixes. Many people do not give credit to the ability of a baby's learning and development, especially at such a young age. Try giving them more credit and see the impact it will make once they are a toddler.

Those are the general changes I found helped avoid bigger issues further down the line. Now I will discuss baby moving into their own room. I was terrified with Anna, because she was my first and seemed so small. I was so nervous about moving her into her own room, and I will be 100% honest, from night one, there were no issues. Anna slept through without a single cry her first night and even moved her wake-up time to 07:30 am. Anna naturally moved her wake time to 07:30 am, which obviously delayed her first bottle, but the rest of her feeds continued at the same time. Always take note of your baby's cues. As baby develops, they may naturally move some of their previous routine. So, Anna's morning bottle was later, but we continued with the rest of her feeds at the previous times, and she was happy with the same.

When moving into their own room, I kept the girls' night routine the same however, I did introduce instrumental lullabies at this time. I think it was due to me being conscious that there would be no noises within the room now that my husband and I were not sharing the room with the baby. So once the baby was placed into bed, I set instrumental lullabies to play on a timer for two hours. Following which, I played pink noise for 40 minutes on the lowest volume setting. I found at times I would play pink noise through parts of the night, if the baby stirred for the first two to three weeks of moving into their own room. I found the pink noise would help baby settle themselves and again make up for the additional sounds/noises that would be missing once in their own room. Be mindful of having the pink noise on the lowest volume setting and do not become dependent on playing any version of white/pink noise as it can be linked with disrupted sleep once the baby is older (toddler). As I said, use it initially when moving rooms, but not long-term.

Molly was more likely to wake up through the night due to needing help to reposition her. Between 6 and 8 months, a baby's ability to move themselves from lying, sitting, and rolling will develop. Initially, I found that both girls would move onto their stomachs to fall asleep, and Molly would wake to be placed onto her back during the night. I also began providing additional docdees at this stage. Due to the baby's limited movement, to help the baby find a doedee I placed two or three doedees around the cot. However, a word of warning, now Molly needs three doedees going to bed, one in her mouth and one in each hand.

Depending on the time of year, when the baby moves to their own room, Anna (November), Molly (March), you can provide a night light. Anna, I set a night light timer for 1 hour. Molly didn't need a night light, as due to it being Spring, it was still bright outside when she was going to bed. Consider the time of year ahead of time. You may need additional blackout blinds (temporary) as well as blackout curtains for the baby's room. It was only now that the baby was in their own room that I pulled both the blinds and curtains at naptime.

I also began playing instrumental lullabies throughout naptime. I'm not sure why it was at this stage other than aiding the move to their individual room. I never had an issue with nap or bedtime. Molly stuck with her 07:00 am wake up until she was about 12 months old, and as I said, Anna moved closer to 07:30 am from 6 months. I did find both girls again had a sleep regression at 8 months and thankfully just with naptime, not bedtime. Like their four-month sleep regression, it passed quickly (3-5 days), and I just continued with their routine as normal.

Another difference I made was regarding the baby's camera/monitor. Both girls have a camera/baby monitor in their room. Once they moved into their own room with Anna, I kept the monitor screen and volume on throughout the night. With Molly, after about one week in her own room, I noticed that she made more noises/sounds throughout her sleep, which caused me to wake throughout the night. She was not making noise out of needing attention or reassurance, she simply just made noises in her sleep. So, I decided to leave the monitor screen on but mute the volume, gasp. But as we all know, camera monitors are not that old an invention. Both girls sleep roughly five feet from my room, therefore I will hear anytime they cry. So, after waking pointlessly for the first week of Molly's move to her own room, I decided to mute the camera volume. Then when I heard her in the night, I could check the camera and decide if I needed to go in. Plus, majority of the time, you will know which cry needs to be responded to without checking the camera.

The weaning process

You will be scared, there is no point saying otherwise, baby has just begun sitting independently, now you must provide food to eat. Don't get yourself into a panic and take your time. Some rush to replace bottles with food, I did not. I will discuss how I replaced bottles for food, but do not rush. Weaning is a whole new process, and the skills required of the baby need to develop throughout this time. Whichever approach you are taking, spoon-feeding or BLW, you will need to support the baby throughout this process. You will need to supervise closely due to choking hazards and educate yourself on how to respond if the baby should choke. If you are going with BLW, research the safer ways to cook and cut food for the baby throughout their first year. Remember not to add salt or sugar to any food, and honey is dangerous for a baby's consumption before 1 year. If you are providing ready-made/processed foods, ensure they are age-appropriate for consumption and review the ingredients before giving them to the baby.

Tip: Introduce highchair to the baby a week or so before starting the weaning process. I simply put the baby into the highchair for a few minutes, each day before we began offering food. I thought this would help the baby to become a little more comfortable with the highchair before suddenly sitting independently to eat.

Offer only one type of food initially, this is all about learning. Choose which food and how to safely prepare it before offering it to the baby. Only provide one or two pieces of the food at a time, do not overwhelm the baby with choices at too young an age. You can work up to different food groups at the same meal over time, but not now. Concentrate on introducing different food textures in the early stages so that the baby gets to experience the same and reduce the chances of pickier eating in the future. I always told baby what they were eating, which bib they had. "Green/blue/pink bib", "green/purple/yellow" cup, as this is a simple way to introduce more vocabulary throughout the day and aid baby's understanding. I provided water in a Sippy cup from day one. Not under any illusion that they would lift the cup and drink from it, but that it was associated with mealtimes from the beginning. The same with cutlery and plates/bowls. From about two weeks into the weaning process, I would tell the baby they had a fork/spoon and demonstrate how to use it. I would provide support intermittently when the baby attempted to use cutlery. I focused on having all mealtime utensils introduced early so that they were always aware of the same and supported their development by using them in time. All food was eaten in a highchair at the dinner table. Again, this has shown such a difference in the long run, we eat sitting at the table, no toys/screens, etc. Which to me is common sense, also I am a big believer in starting as you mean to go on. I hear people complaining all the time that their toddler won't sit at the table. If it's always been that way, then there's no later battle to be had.

How I began Weaning

I started introducing food before the 10:00 am bottle. It is often advised to try to offer food before the baby is too hungry or too full. I found that ten or fifteen minutes before a bottle feed was due worked well for both my girls. You may need to play about with the timing of offering food. At 09:45 am, I would put the baby into their highchair with a sippy cup of water and a bib, then give them a small portion of food. I started with banana, eggs, toast, a pancake, Greek yoghurt, strawberries, and sweet potato. Provide one food to begin with, show the baby how to eat it and then place it in front of them. I began with high allergy foods in week one. Now I'm lucky there are no known allergies in our family, but you never know. I would always introduce a 'high risk' allergy food at 09:45 am feed, as this allowed time for the reaction to be spotted and responded to.

Replacing bottles with Food

I did not replace any of the girls' bottle feeds with food until they were 8 months old. Between the ages of 6-12 months, babies will still require a minimum of 500 ml of formula. So, depending on the size (oz's) and number of bottle feeds, you will need to consider this requirement before replacing bottle feeds with food. As well as the formula requirements, I also found that giving the baby this time enabled them to grow in ability, skills and confidence to self-feed and then reduce/replace the bottle with a meal.

Both Anna and Molly replaced their 10:00 am and 16:00 bottle with food by nine months old. Their 13:00 bottle became solid lunch by about 10/11 months and then their 07:30 and 19:00 feeds remained in place until after 12 months. With both Molly and Anna, they simply switched from morning bottle feed to breakfast. Once they were 1 year and 1 week, I brought them downstairs for breakfast, no issues.

The only bottles I found that where a little harder to replace were lunchtime and bedtime, both feeds before sleep. So, with the lunchtime bottle (13:00), I found I needed to reduce the bottles' oz to build up to replacing, same for food. I took the approach of providing their meal first, and then over a few days, reduced their bottle from 7 oz to 4 oz. Then after about two/three days of the 4 oz bottle, just provided the meal, then went for a nap. With bedtime (19:00), I took away this bottle at 14 months. I think we are all nervous of taking away the bedtime bottle in fear of ruining the baby's ability to sleep through the night. But it needs to be removed before the baby becomes dependent on that bottle to get to sleep. So once the baby was 1 year old, I began providing supper at 18:00. This usually consisted of toast and banana or porridge and banana and reducing the oz's in their 19:00 feed. Once the bottle consisted of only 4 oz, I would then try to put the baby down to sleep and not return with the bottle to see their response. Molly's first attempt was the last, she did not look for her 19:00 bottle. Anna took two attempts. First night, I didn't return with the bottle, and she cried for about five minutes, so we went back up with the bottle. Five nights later, I did the same again, put her down to sleep and waited for her response. Anna did not look for the bottle, so that was that, we were done with bottle feeds.

Baby's Development

Baby's physical development between 6-9 months is amazing. They will now be sitting independently, using facial expressions and babbling much more. Baby may have begun holding their sippy cup, utensils and clapping. Continue to provide support for the baby's development through nursery rhymes with hand movements for them to copy. Demonstrate waving for bye-bye and hello. You will need to support them in putting weight onto their legs, which simply means holding the baby in a standing position on your knees and allowing them to support their body weight for short periods. You can also help the baby learn to crawl by crawling yourself to demonstrate and try to get them to follow you. There are also different toys that can be used to support the baby to crawl. For example, a toy with wheels can be pushed by the baby for them to crawl after. Or simply continue to place a toy further away from the baby when they are in a crawling position to encourage them to move forward. Balls are always a great option for a baby to reach for and crawl after as the object continues to move forward majority of the time, encouraging the baby to follow. Once the baby has begun to crawl, they will most likely begin to stand up assisted. Usually starting with furniture walking and reaching for objects higher up, e.g. the coffee table or chair. Now is the time to ensure there are no dangerous or breakable objects in baby's reach as they will begin to lift and grab everything.

By about 8 months, you will most likely need to fit stair gates and cupboard locks throughout your home. Baby's mobility will be on the fast track now, and they want to explore everywhere. Separation anxiety can also be common at 8months of age and is perfectly normal. Baby will be more aware of where they are and who is with them. I took the approach of telling baby ahead of time that "mummy has to go; Nanny will be here and then Mummy will be back". Now obviously baby had no clue what I was talking about at this age but again it was introducing the language. That could later be attached to an action which baby would understand in the not-so-distant future. Many people told me "To just go, when the baby was distracted", and I never took this approach. Baby's biggest fear is mum/dad disappearing, so I chose not to do this. I always told baby when I was going, and now, they are both toddlers, there is no issue with Mum/Dad having to leave them with grandparents, etc.

9 – 12 months

Our Routine at this age:

07:30: Wake time and first feed (bottle).

07:30-08:30: Coffee/breakfast, floor time with toys/books, shower, get baby dressed and a new nappy.

First Nap: 09:00 Molly (dropped her nap by 11 months). Anna, 09:30. I would get dressed and have a coffee during nap.

10:00: Snack – banana/yoghurt/pancake/apple/homemade cereal bar or muffin

10:30/10:45: Get out of the house, whether it was for a walk, class, or visiting friends/family.

12:30/12:45: Home and Lunch – toast/eggs/sweet potato/cheese/chicken/veg

13:00/15:00: Afternoon nap– we <u>all</u> napped.

15:00: Wake up from nap

15:30/15:45: Snack – rice cakes/strawberries/raisins/grapes/crackers/pasta

16:30-18:00: Floor-time/play with toys/books, and sometimes another walk. All electronics are off throughout the house.

18:00-18:30: Wind down before bedtime routine, baby would complete my bedtime routine i.e. clean my face, get jammies on. Set up their bedtime so nightlight on instead of main bedroom light, instrumental music on low. Nappy and baby-grow, onsie, sleep bag all laid out and ready to go.

18:30: I would bring the baby upstairs to get ready for bed. Change their clothes and nappy, talking softly, reminding them throughout that it's bedtime. Close to 11 months, I would introduce books and floor time to the baby's bedtime routine. As bottles were now consumed quickly, and soon the bedtime bottle would be gone. So, I would expand on the bedtime routine. Will discuss the same in this section.

18:55: Placed into their cot-bed. End of talking.

19:00: Return to complete the last feed. Set night light on 1-hour timer.

19:30: Baby is placed into bed for the night, set instrumental lullabies to play for 2 hours on very low volume. Anna had a night light, and Molly did not. Say ni-night and leave.

Sleep Routine Adjustments

Baby's routine is set, there are no changes to sleep or feeding times at this stage, just merely adaptations made. As you can see, the baby is down to 2 bottles per day, all other feeds are solid food. The lunchtime bottle became food around month 10 for both my girls.

Bedtime will need to be adapted once the baby gets to around 10/11 months as their routine expands past just having a bottle. When I brought the baby up to bed to get changed, I introduced floor time. At this stage most babies will be furniture-walking and crawling without issue. So, after getting changed for bed, I would simply sit on the floor with the baby, read books, play with teddies, and crawl around the floor. Then once it was 18:55, place them into their sleep bag, say "ni night time, mummy going to get bottle", dim their night light and end of talking. Return with bottle, offer feed in the rocking chair, keep them upright for a minute or two after the bottle. There is no need for winding after 6 months. I always just felt more comfortable still having the baby upright a few minutes after finishing their bottle. I may have sung a song whilst holding the baby from this stage as the last sign of going to bed. As the baby will have had a consistent routine from week 6 for preparing and going to bed, you can add in a little song, nursery rhyme, whatever, at this point. As the same is not required to get to sleep, but you might like to do something to mark going to bed.

Morning nap, the average age for baby to drop their morning nap can range from 10 to 14 months of age. And of course, my girls were complete opposite ends of the scale for this milestone. However, I took the same approach with both. Molly dropped her nap between 10 and 11 months of age. The rule of thumb is to continue to offer the nap and once the baby has skipped the nap continuously for two weeks, it's gone. So once Molly had decided she was done with the morning nap, I got her dressed at 09:00, played soft music in her room, gave her teddy and books, doedee and placed her into her cot-bed. Told her "Mummy is going to get a shower and dressed", I left the bedroom door open and left the room. Initially, she may have amused herself for ten minutes, then cried out so I would go back in to reassure her, tell her I was going to get dressed and leave her again. Both girls were happy to amuse themselves for another ten minutes, then cry out. I would come back and lift them out initially after 20 minutes, but over time this has increased to 35 minutes. With more books, teddies, and Toni boxes being introduced. But the skill of independent play has allowed this 'free time' for me to wash, dress, maybe even grab a coffee. Do not panic once the morning nap is dropped. Replace the previous naptime with independent play time in the baby's room and this will develop further once the baby becomes a toddler.

Baby's Development

It may be surprising, but by 9 months old, you may find the use of the word "no" being introduced. Baby is gaining both mobility and confidence in exploring the world. You will need to ensure the baby's surroundings are safe and removed from hazards that may now be in baby's reach.

There are many changes to a baby's physical abilities during months 9-12. Most likely, the baby will begin standing, furniture walking and building up to those first independent steps. Both my girls walked independently before their first birthday. Pay attention to supporting the baby during these physical developments, do not get carried away with equipment. The easiest way to support a baby is to allow them to be barefoot where possible, allow them to furniture walk with supervision and be mindful of which 'walking apparatus' you use. The most effective and safest is a baby push-along walker. Do not get baby a seated walker with wheels. This does not support their ability to walk and is banned in several countries due to safety concerns when using the same.

Baby's communication will be expanding, and they may begin to distinguish babbling into words. Ensure you respond to the baby's babbling to show you are listening and repeat back words you think they may be saying. If possible, point to what it is you think they are trying to say, e.g. "the cup" hold/point to the cup. Baby may also begin using hand signs to identify nursery rhymes or want more food. Once the baby begins making attempts at words, keep the sentences you are saying to them short. For example, "want more yoghurt", "want more water", this will support the baby to understand the purpose of words and differentiate between objects. Use direct instructions, and continue to keep sentences short, "get the ball", "get the book".

By 12 months, you can begin to add a little description to short sentences. Especially when reading books with baby "that's the blue cup", ask questions as well. Baby may not be able to tell you where the dog is but ask "where's the dog" and see if they can point to it on the page. Asking questions, repeating words and describing colours/shapes will encourage the baby to use vocabulary as they will naturally mirror the example you set.

And just like that baby is turning one year old. You won't believe how quickly time has gone and how much both you and baby have grown. You did it. Now onto toddlerhood… it's amazing.

Final Note

I hope motherhood is everything you wished and dreamed it to be, but if it's not, that's okay. We can only imagine and try to plan for what's going to happen, which usually doesn't work out anyway. There is an element of just wait and see. There will be days when everything is fantastic, and you are loving life. And there will be other days when you feel like you have no idea what you are doing or how to make it to the end of the day. That is normal, no one can be at the top of their game constantly. Motherhood is hard, ensure you have a support person/people. Check in with yourself, especially in the early weeks. Make sure you are just having a bad morning or a tired day, and if you feel it could be anything more, speak with medical professions.

You will lose yourself completely those first few months, and that's okay. That's what's supposed to happen. I feel in this social-media-crazed world, there is so much coverage, pressure and expectations that women should bounce back to who they were automatically and continue being the same person they were before becoming a mother. Which is ridiculous, you may only manage a shower and to put on some gym/comfy clothes in the initial few months. I didn't feel much like myself again until Anna was about 8 months old. By that stage, I was pregnant again anyway, so back to the start I went. You won't ever go back to the same version of yourself, how could you?

"When you are a mother, you are never really alone in your thoughts. A mother always has to think twice, once for herself and once for her child." - **Sophia Loren**.

Motherhood has a way of erasing parts of who you used to be and allowing you to explore a new version of yourself. What you may lose initially when becoming a mother will be replaced by something so much better and more beautiful than you could have imagined. Time goes so quickly, so the weekends away, dinners out you may be skipping now will come back around before you know it. Do not panic about only having time for your family, that's how it's supposed to be. Please, please, please do not compare yourself to other mothers, especially on social media. You figure out what type of mother and woman you want to be. What works for your family and don't judge yourself on others' perception or expectations. When you're at home, you're at home, so leave others' opinions at the door, however you choose to live and raise your child.

With love,
Emma.

www.ingramcontent.com/pod-product-compliance
Lightning Source LLC
Chambersburg PA
CBHW061232070526
44584CB00030B/4094